Lloyd Alexander

Twayne's United States Authors Series

Children's Literature

Ruth K. MacDonald, Editor
Purdue University Calumet

TUSAS 576

LLOYD ALEXANDER
Courtesy of Alexander Limont

Lloyd Alexander

Jill P. May
Purdue University

Twayne Publishers • Boston
A Division of G. K. Hall & Co.

Lloyd Alexander
Jill P. May

Copyright © 1991 by G. K. Hall & Co.
All rights reserved.
Published by Twayne Publishers
A Division of G. K. Hall & Co.
70 Lincoln Street
Boston, Massachusetts 02111

Typeset in 10/13 Century Schoolbook by Compset, Inc., of Beverly, Massachusetts

10 9 8 7 6 5 4 3 2 1

Library of Congress Cataloging-in-Publication Data

May, Jill P.
    Lloyd Alexander / Jill P. May.
        p.   cm.—(Twayne's United States authors series ; TUSAS
    576. Children's literature)
    Includes bibliographical references and index.
    ISBN 0-8057-7622-2
    1. Alexander, Lloyd—Criticism and interpretation.   2. Children's
literature, American—History and criticism.   I. Title.
II. Series: Twayne's United States authors series ; TUSAS 576.
III. Series: Twayne's United States authors series. Children's
literature.
PS3551.L35698Z77   1991
813' .54—dc20   90-20503
                                                                        CIP

*For the dreamers—
who have given my life
a sense of reality*

Contents

Preface

Although Lloyd Alexander is one of the most significant twentieth-century children's authors, and has been favorably reviewed since he wrote his first children's book, no one has attempted to publish a full-length study of his work until now. No one has written critical discussions of his work as a children's biographer; all of the published scholarship deals with his fantasy books.

Lloyd Alexander's work has long been acknowledged as outstanding. He has won a number of literary awards and has been a featured speaker at several professional meetings of librarians, teachers, and professors working in children's literature. Perhaps because he is congenial and open about his writing, he has been taken less seriously than he should be. His work has been called fine fantasy writing, and he has been compared to the earlier great fantasy authors J. R. R. Tolkien and C. S. Lewis as well as literary fairy-tale author Hans Christian Andersen. Yet, Lloyd Alexander cannot be labeled simply an author of fantasy.

Critics who refuse to look beyond the style of his first highly acclaimed series, the Prydain books, and acknowledge the stylistic divergence of his later works express disappointment in some of his later writings. They make the mistake of defining his accomplishments by the books that fit within the fantasy genre. However, Lloyd Alexander's work can never be evaluated by the yardstick of his first series. He does not rewrite the same stories. In fact, he varies his prose, largely because his message and his style are affected by new experiences, different literary goals. I have tried to deal with the complexity of Alexander's style in my discussion, concentrating on how his writing evolved as he determined to write an altogether different group of books once he seemed to have perfected a particular style.

After I agreed to write the book, I contacted Lloyd and asked if he would be willing to be my first reader. Based on past experience, I knew that he would answer my questions about his rationale for creating a particular book without demanding that my evaluations be approved by him. Biographical information and information concerning awards have been verified by Alexander.

This volume deals with the question of Alexander's style, his success as a writer for contemporary children, and his persistent need to change his writing style. Because he has written with several voices, I have chosen to isolate the works by subject matter and by writing technique. My explanation of how each group of past works relates to subsequent books is based upon scholarly supposition.

Alexander's reputation rests largely on his contribution to children's literature. And, since this book is a part of a series dealing with twentieth-century children's authors, I have chosen to discuss only his children's publications. His earlier translations of French authors and his adult books, however, did lay the groundwork for his later children's stories, and, when applicable, I have commented on these publications. Throughout the book I have attempted to show that Alexander's writing results from his past reading and his memories of Philadelphia and American history, as well as the France and Wales he remembers from World War II. With an eye on the past, Alexander has cautiously viewed the present while looking toward the future with a hope that there will be a more global and humane civilization.

Alexander's children's novels contain a good deal of political philosophy, a theme carefully developed in the following discussion. His desire to tell a good story has always kept him from preaching morals to young readers; yet the morals are there, and I explore them in the following chapters.

Alexander's body of works has caused this critic to consider several pertinent topics in the field of literary criticism. His biographical books suggest that fiction and history are closely linked whenever the audience is children. His Westmark series demonstrates that an author can write a psychological story for young readers and that heroes can be redefined within today's fiction.

His development of strong female characters suggests that feminist theory must consider how twentieth-century male authors view the female as heroine. I have addressed the critical questions that most intrigue me when I am reading Alexander. I hope these issues will be explored by others, as they are central to our understanding of children's literature. In the end, Alexander's work and the lack of critical response has caused me to consider the field of criticism, to evaluate why his works have not been more carefully analyzed.

Once I had written a chapter, I handed it over to my husband, Robert E. May, for copy editing and clarity of ideas.

I have journeyed four times to Alexander's house for research conferences. Janine Alexander has cooked more than her share of dinners during these visits, and I owe her a debt of thanks.

This book is somewhat of a collaborative effort. However, the shape of the arguments, the tone of writing, and the critical interpretations and evaluations are mine alone. I owe a great deal of thanks to both Lloyd Alexander and my husband, Bob, for their continual support.

I also must thank Purdue University's School of Education for its continual support, and my secretaries Bonnie Nowakowski and Jackie Conaway, without whom I would never have completed my work. Finally, I must commend my daughters Beth and Heather for reading Lloyd's books, discussing the project with me, and demanding that I sit down and write when I felt more inclined to work on something that seemed more immediately pressing.

Chronology

1959 *Janine Is French* (adult book). Receives the Jewish Book Council Isaac Seigel Award for *Border Hawk.*

1960 *My Love Affair with Music* (adult book); *The Flagship Hope: Aaron Lopez.*

1962 *Park Avenue Vet,* with Louis J. Camuti (adult book).

1963 *Time Cat: The Remarkable Journeys of Jason and Gareth.*

1964 *The Book of Three;* American Library Association Notable Book. *Fifty Years in the Doghouse* (adult book).

1965 *The Black Cauldron;* Newbery Award runner-up. *Coll and His White Pig.*

1966 *The Castle of Llyr.*

1967 *Taran Wanderer. The Truthful Harp.* Author-in-residence at Springfield school system, Delaware County, Pennsylvania.

1968 *The High King.*

1969 *The Truthful Harp* named to the *Horn Book* Best Books for Children. *The High King* wins the Newbery Award.

1970 *The Marvelous Misadventures of Sebastian.* Begins four-year stint as author-in-residence at Temple University in Philadelphia.

1971 *The King's Fountain. The Marvelous Misadventures of Sebastian* wins the children's National Book Award.

1972 *The Four Donkeys.* Receives the Drexel University Citation for Excellence.

1973 *The Cat Who Wished to Be a Man. The Foundling and Tales of Prydain.* Alexander appointed to *Cricket* magazine's editorial advisory board.

1974 Appointed to the library committee, *World Book Encyclopedia.*

1975 *The Wizard in the Tree.*

1976 Receives the Pennsylvania School Librarians Award of Recognition.

1977 *The Town Cats and Other Tales.*

1978 *The First Two Lives of Lukas-Kasha.*

1981 *Westmark;* American Library Association Notable Book. Receives the Netherlands Silver Slate Pencil Award and the Austrian Children's Book Prize for *The First Two Lives of Lukas-Kasha.*

1982 *The Kestrel;* Parents' Choice Award. *Westmark* wins the American Book Award in Children's Literature. Begins serving on the board of directors for Friends of International Board on Books for Youth. Receives the Keystone State Reading Association Literary Award.

1984 *The Beggar Queen;* American Library Association Best Book for Young Adults. Received the Swedish Golden Cat Award.

1985 Disney animated film *The Black Cauldron.* Citation of Recognition by the Pennsylvania House of Representatives.

1986 *The Illyrian Adventure;* American Library Association Notable Book and Parents' Choice Award. Receives the Regina Medal for Contributions to Children's Literature.

1987 *The El Dorado Adventure. The Town Cats* receives the Norwegian Children's Book Award. Alexander receives the Helen Keating Ott Award from the Church and Synagogue Library Association and the Pennsylvania Library Association Carolyn W. Field Medal.

1988 *The Drackenberg Adventure.*

1989 *The Jedera Adventure.*

1990 *The Philadelphia Adventure.*

1

Bringing the Past and
the Future into the Present

"Yes," Geriant answered willingly, "altogether true.
Sorcery is not by birthright. I have no inborn powers. The birds you saw? Not doves, but only bits of
white parchment. The flowers? Dry grass and tinted
leaves. The stars? A handful of bright pebbles. I only
helped you imagine these things to be more than
what they are. If this pleased you for a few minutes,
I could ask for nothing better."[1]

Although Geriant is a fictional hero in one of Lloyd Alexander's
stories, he speaks for the author himself. Geriant tells the reader
what Alexander believes: it is the writer's responsibility to depict
an illusionary world that allows the reader to see his world in a
different way. It is the author's responsibility to encourage the
reader to consider alternative thoughts and dreams. What makes
Lloyd Alexander create new worlds for the reader to explore? Why
does he insist on seeing more in his world than the average person sees?

Philadelphia Childhood

From his early childhood on, Lloyd Alexander saw the world differently from the rest of his family. Born in Philadelphia in 1924,

Alexander did not grow up in a literary family interested in reading. His father was busy keeping his family fed, housed, and clothed. Alexander had little to do with his sister, who was five years older. A child who lived in a home that continually housed drop-in relatives, he spent much of his time alone. His mother was always supportive, but she was not interested in having long conversations with her son. Alexander began to entertain himself at an early age.

Although none of his immediate family members was a reader, his father bought a large collection of books to fill the family bookshelves. Somewhere between the ages of three and four, Alexander "broke the reading code" and began to read on his own. His ability to read isolated him even further from the rest of his family. Alexander's father viewed his reading as a curiosity, and he and his wife used Lloyd's early precocity to entertain company. Alexander loved reading, but he hated having to perform for people he hardly knew.

Born in Kingston, Jamaica, Alexander's father and his brother had moved to the United States while they were teenagers. A shrewd businessman, Alan Alexander prospered as a stockbroker while Lloyd was young. The Alexander family lived in Drexel Hill, a pleasant upper-middle-class suburb of Philadelphia.

When Alexander was old enough to enter school his father sent him to the Friends Elementary School, a private Quaker school, and, later, to Friends Central. Alexander quickly tested out of the first and second grades and entered third grade. He was smaller than the other third graders and was bullied by his classmates. The school believed in developing the total child, but Alexander could not keep up with the physical activities common for his older classmates.

Alexander's early neighborhood friends enjoyed playing imaginary games of cowboys and Indians and concocting "formulas" with their newly acquired science kits. Some of his playmates had fathers who had recently returned from World War I, bringing home various pieces of military equipment. Alexander and the other boys used this wartime paraphernalia when they played "World War I." Thus, as he grew up Alexander thought of war as a wonderful adventure; he dreamed of the heroism found in wartime and failed to recognize its more somber aspects.

When Alexander was eight, his father lost his money, and Alexander began attending public school. Once again, he was tested to see what grade he should be attending, and once again he skipped a grade. At age nine Lloyd Alexander was a seventh grader. He preferred the public school to the private Quaker schools, largely because he was not subjected to the same kinds of harassment. In the public school he had five classmates who had skipped grades, and they bonded together.

During these early years Alexander began to read about King Arthur. He also loved Charles Dickens and had a favorite practical book, *The Century Dictionary: An Encyclopedic Lexicon of the English Language*. Alexander pored over the illustrations, looked up all the new words he found while reading, and eventually stuffed the dictionary full of mementos.

When Alexander entered the area's academic high school, he felt that learning became tedious. At times he feigned illness so that he could miss school. He once confessed, "My greatest triumph [in convincing others of his illnesses] came on the eve of a geography examination on some impassioned subject like the imports and exports of Tierra del Fuego, when I was able to present our family doctor with all the classic symptoms of malaria; a remarkable achievement since not one anopheles mosquito had ever been sighted in Drexel Hill." He went on to say, "When eventually I came to write fantasy, this training in practical imagination stood me in good stead."[2]

Alexander's high school interests and reading expanded, and his goals changed. When he was thirteen he announced to his family that he would like to become an Episcopal priest. Although his parents were doctrinaire enough to suspect the religious attitudes of all other churches, they were not interested in having a clergyman in the family. Neither his father nor his mother supported his decision. By age fifteen Alexander announced that he hoped to become a poet, but his father advised him to forget poetry and go to work when he graduated from high school. And so, in May 1940, he accepted a job as an office boy at a local bank.

During work hours he ran errands for the staff; at night he read and tried his hand at writing. One of his first published adult books, *And Let the Credit Go,* humorously recounts his early experiences.

Alexander liked some of his English classes in high school and hoped to attend college in order to study literature, become a teacher, and eventually write. Since he was still living at home he was able to save three dollars out of his ten-dollar weekly wages for his college education. When it became apparent that he really intended to go to school, his parents agreed to help him enter West Chester College. Alexander could live at home and travel to classes, taking the trolley line at the bottom of the hill. He entered college in September 1941 and tested out of a year's worth of education. Although the literature classes were advanced ones, the lessons seemed boring and mundane. His only enjoyable first-year learning experience came early each morning when he raced into his French class after his hour's commute on the trolley.

Alexander's attitudes were shared by another commuter, and they banded together. Both held the hope that the next year would be better. When Alexander returned to college the next fall, he and his friend looked at their schedules and mutually agreed to quit. "When we saw what we were in for," he says, "we left our books, schedules, and padlocks behind and walked out. We were so relieved to be free from the prospects of another year of poorly taught classes that we never asked for our fees to be returned."

War Experiences

Just after his nineteenth birthday Alexander decided to join the U.S. Army. His reasons for joining were ambiguous. He knew that he would probably be drafted soon, and he wanted to save someone else from going into the military. He also wanted to help with the war efforts; some of that childhood play with World War I gas masks and helmets made him see war as glorious. However, he knew that everyone would not return home a victorious hero. Fear, hope, and patriotism were intermingled.

His early career in the service was full of disappointments. While he was in basic training he was assigned to be an artilleryman. His job was to load the howitzers, but the heavy shells were cumbersome and difficult for Alexander to manipulate. He kept dropping them as he tried to load the gun. Realizing that Alexander would be a handicap at the front, the army transferred him to the medic division. The sight of blood made him faint. Once more Alexander was transferred, this time to the Army Band. Since he was without any previous experience in marching bands, Alexander soon lost his new occupation. He was reassigned to the chaplin as an assistant and might have remained for some time if he had wanted. He humorously admits that he seemed able to clean up the chapel and play the organ. However, he was also assigned kitchen duty, a job detested by all, and so he wanted out. One day, he saw a sign posted in the kitchen. The army wanted to establish a special corps of men who could speak foreign languages. Alexander was fluent in French, so he applied. Immediately, his life in the service changed.

Alexander was reassigned to the military intelligence and was sent for intensive training in French culture, European history, topography of France, and foreign language at Lafayette College in Pennsylvania. These courses were challenging. Alexander enjoyed his studies during the week and commuted to Philadelphia to party on the weekend.

Within four months he was transferred to a special training camp in the mountains. Alexander recalls that the camp was filled with authors, artists, and young politicians. "It was heaven," he explains. "All of the misfits were in one camp together. The spit and polish was gone. It was a different kind of military experience." The days were filled with classes in several languages followed by difficult tests. Those who failed were shipped out. In addition, the men were sent out on grueling field exercises. Because they were being trained to work with the partisans, they were expected to fight, help with military strategy, and lead military maneuvers.

At the end of three months the men who had made it through the training period were given a final test, commissioned, and sent off to duty. Alexander recalls, "My hopes for adventure brightened. . . . Rumors flew that we would be parachuted into France to work with the Resistance. . . . Instead, we sailed to England, and in late autumn, we were ordered to Wales to be outfitted for combat." For six weeks of that autumn in 1944 Alexander commuted between Staffordshire and Wales. He was immediately attracted to the country's people and terrain. He remembers it as a "land far more ancient than England, wilder and rougher hewn. . . . Wales, to my eyes appeared still a realm of bards and heroes; even the coal-tips towered like dark fortresses."[3] Alexander's short experience in Wales would later inspire him to write his first fantasy series.

By December Alexander had been assigned to Alsace-Lorraine. He spent the winter in the Vosges mountains, and his ambivalent feelings about war and bravery returned. The bravado in him made him ask to be left behind to defend the line alone against the Germans, but the caution in him made him realize that death was always nearby. At one point he and a friend were escorting an officer back to his company after his hospital release when the jeep they were in crashed on a mountain road. Alexander's nose was broken, his buddy's ribs were broken, and their comrade-in-arms went into shock. It was night, the road was bitter cold, and their jeep was ruined. To Alexander, their rescue was like a dream. "Suddenly troops arrived. They were Americans, but they spoke Spanish. I believe that they were Puerto Ricans, but I'm not sure. I must have passed out because I remember telling them where we were going, and then I don't remember anything until I was back in the barracks." Once healed, Alexander went with his company into Germany. With the signing of the peace treaty, he was reassigned to Paris.

Paris

In many ways Paris was a turning point in Alexander's literary career. While stationed there, he met the woman he would marry, visited with Gertrude Stein, and agreed to translate the poet Paul Eluard. Alexander was stationed as a counterintelligence translator, but during the autumn of 1945 he was busy driving jeeps and trying to write. He knew that Gertrude Stein lived in Paris, was kind to American soldiers, and was a friend of American authors Ernest Hemingway and F. Scott Fitzgerald. He was also aware that she was as strong a critic of formal schooling as he was, and so he decided to meet her. Young and bold, Alexander looked up her phone number and called her on the telephone. She invited him over for the first of several visits. Years later he wrote about the experience, saying:

> When I confessed I hoped to be a writer, she nodded and answered, "Yes, if that's what you really want, then you will be."
>
> But she warned me it would be difficult. She told me how discouraging it had been for her, how long she had worked before publishing anything—and then only to be severely criticized. . . .
>
> I remember her giving me a book during one of our afternoons, signing the flyleaf for me and adding, "May it be as good as he hopes." . . . What she gave me was an understanding that art and literature don't magically appear on museum walls and library bookshelves. They're the work of real women and men who lived in the real world.[4]

Stein liked to encourage young authors, but she was also quick to dismiss the irresponsible and untalented. She must have sensed that Alexander was sincere. Their casual friendship had less to do with literature than it did with the sharing of dreams and desires. Stein gave Alexander the courage to believe that he could be an author.

Alexander struck up a different kind of friendship with Paul Eluard. Again, he resorted to the phone book and made a telephone call. Alexander admired Eluard's surrealistic poetry; at this point in his life he wanted to write in the same style. When he first came to visit Eluard he brought along some of Eluard's poems that he had translated. Eluard was impressed with his work and asked if Alexander would be his English translator. A friendship based on professional interests ensued as Alexander worked on the translations. To him Eluard was a living example of what a writer could be: one who wrote beautifully and feelingly about things that mattered. He was also a person to admire because he had actively worked in the French Resistance. Alexander's translations of Eluard's work were published by New Directions in 1951. He also translated two works by Jean-Paul Sartre and one by Paul Vialar.

Most of Alexander's life in France has appeared in his books in one way or another. The humorous and romantic parts can be found in his early semiautobiographical adult novels. In one, *Janine Is French,* he says, "I met Janine for the first time during the summer following the war, on the Boulevard Haussman, in the worst rainstorm of the season. She was on her way home from shopping, and I offered her a lift in my army jeep."[5] Janine had lived through the hardest parts of war. She had a ten-year-old daughter, Madeleine, and Alexander began to court her also. He picked her up from boarding school and took her to the coffee shops. He bought her little things that Janine could not afford because of the war. Four months after their first meeting, on 8 January 1946, Alexander and Janine were married. They settled into a small one-room apartment. Alexander attended classes at the Sorbonne, more determined than ever to be an author. When his duty was over, he returned to his old neighborhood in Philadelphia with his new family.

A Philadelphia Author

The Philadelphia in which they lived was entrenched in its history and conservative in attitudes. Alexander's parents viewed Catholics negatively; they did not speak French. Yet, they opened their home to Alexander and his new family. Janine has said that they especially loved Madeleine. A young adolescent, she was in love with her new country, eagerly learning English, and enjoying new customs. Janine was less enamored with her new life. These early years have been humorously depicted in *Janine Is French*. They relate Janine's early efforts to make money by sewing, the loss of their child through a miscarriage, and their eventual move to an old house in need of repair. Little by little the house was fixed up, cats were acquired, and the family settled down to a "typical" routine.

An aspiring author's typical routine is quite different from anyone else's, and Lloyd's was no exception. In the early years when he was trying to write while supporting his family, Alexander worked as an advertising copywriter, layout artist, cartoonist, and magazine editor during the day. During the early morning hours and late at night he wrote and read. He was forced to keep up this strenuous schedule until 1971 when his earnings as a published author allowed him to pursue writing full time.

Prior to his turning to children's literature, Alexander had hoped for a very different kind of writing career. He wanted to write for adults, and he began by writing adult novels about Philadelphia. Although Alexander had lived most of his life in Philadelphia, the city he depicted in his early writings had little to do with his childhood or adult experiences. He later admitted that these early writings were disasters, and added, "imagination does have its limits."

His best early writing was the short story "The Fantastic Symphony," which was published in the *New Directions Annual* in 1949. This serious story closely resembles some of the surrealistic pieces he had admired. It is based on lines from Hector Berlioz's "Notes on La Symphonie Fantastique" and focuses on imagery. In this piece he expresses both his growing animosity toward war and his fascination with music. These two themes continually surface in his writings for children.

By the time he published his early adult novels his style had changed. His writing began to contain detailed characterization, a great deal of humor, and an optimistic overtone. These elements are consistently found in his books for children.

Writing for Children

It was not until the early sixties that Lloyd Alexander turned his back on the adult marketplace. He sensed a feeling of despair in adult fiction and began to believe that there was little future in writing it. His own pessimistic outlook was tempered with his wry sense of humor and his ability to see the possibilities in real life situations. Alexander did not isolate himself from the real world or give up hope that the world could be a better place. He wrote optimistically, even in the darkest hours of Vietnam, a time that troubled him a great deal. However, as the years have gone by he has changed his attitudes about society. The gradual swing from optimism to despair back to a cautious optimism is shown in the plots and themes of his books for children.

Alexander's attitudes about war have changed since he was a boy playing with the World War I gas masks. He now regards war as a poor answer to problems and says that no war was ever ultimately good. Although he believes that the United States was right to fight in World War II, he does not feel that U.S. involvement in Vietnam was necessary or good. In the spring of 1970 he wrote, "Each day of war takes us farther from all we could hope to be or to do. . . . Our lives erode and diminish, our children see no future except a calendar of anguish and death. Our only hope for tomorrow is peace now."[6]

He remains interested in children and concerned about their future. He wishes to keep his readers in mind when he is writing and to have contact with them. Alexander answers fan letters, allows classes to visit him in his home, and has kept in touch with some of his readers throughout their lives. In 1967–68 he visited with many of the youngsters in the Springfield school system in Delaware County, Pennsylvania, while serving as author-in-residence. He has picketed with children as a promotional device in front of the Philadelphia Free Library, visited several schools throughout the United States, and participated in many librarian/teacher/author workshops and programs. During 1970–74 he worked as author-in-residence at Temple University.

His opinions as a critic and a philosopher are highly respected.

He has spoken to audiences of children's literature specialists at the American Library Association, the Children's Literature Association, the International Reading Association, and the National Council of Teachers of English. In addition, he has served on the editorial boards of *World Book Encyclopedia, Cricket Magazine, The Advocate,* and the Friends of International Board on Books for Youth.

Awards

Lloyd Alexander has been continually recognized as an outstanding author of children's literature. He has won most of the prestigious children's book awards given in the United States. *Border Hawk* received the Jewish Book Council Award in 1959; *The Book of Three* was a 1964 American Library Association Notable Book; *The Black Cauldron* was runner-up for the 1965 Newbery Award; *The Truthful Harp* was named to the 1969 *Horn Book* Best Books for Children; *The High King* won the 1969 Newbery Award; *The Marvelous Misadventures of Sebastian* won the children's National Book Award in 1971; *Westmark* won the American Book Award in Children's Literature in 1982. He has also been recognized by professional organizations and has been given the Drexel University Citation for Excellence, the Pennsylvania School Librarians' Award of Recognition, the Church and Synagogue Library Association's Helen Keating Ott Award, and the Catholic Library Association's Regina Medal for continued outstanding contribution to children's literature.

He is equally well known in other parts of the world and has won awards in other countries. *The First Two Lives of Lukas-Kasha* won the 1981 Netherlands Silver Slate Pencil Award and the Austrian Children's Book Award; *The Beggar Queen* received the 1984 Swedish Golden Cat Award; *The Town Cats and Other Tales* received the 1987 Norwegian Children's Book Award. His books are found in several countries, including England, the Netherlands, Canada, France, Japan, Austria, Norway, and Sweden. During the summer of 1989 the Japanese Children's Theatre presented an adaptation of *The Cat Who Wished to Be a Man* on all of the islands.

Alexander Today

As an author who maintains a structured writing schedule, Alexander relishes his solitude when he is involved in a project. His wife, Janine, once commented that she always looks forward to the completion of a project because it usually brings a break in their schedule and allows them to relax with friends and family. Between those breaks Alexander keeps a rigorous daily schedule. He arises at 4 A.M. and works through the late afternoon hours. For Lloyd Alexander there is really only one meal a day—a fine French repast at the end of his writing when he can share his ideas and concerns with his wife. Even when he is uninspired he continues his routine. Each book requires hours of thinking and planning long before he begins to write. He strongly believes in self-discipline, saying, "You can't rely on inspiration. You make it happen."

Those who have met Lloyd Alexander comment that he looks like a character from one of his books come alive. Some have likened him to Hans Christian Andersen. Genial and friendly, there is nothing pretentious about this children's author. He speaks honestly and with intelligence in his conversations and his writings. He is a slight, gentle man who began his stories using an already established body of legends, literary patterns, and character types to tell a new kind of tale, a twentieth-century tale that would entertain contemporary children's audiences. Alexander is content to write for children because he knows that adults will read the stories with the children and will see the realities of human behavior in his writing. Together, he maintains, they can explore the problems facing them. Concerning his love for writing children's fantasy he once wrote, "Scratch a hard-shelled realist and find a lover of fairy-tales? Maybe. . . . Whatever the merits of the end result, I have never been so caught up in a work, nor loved working as much as I have in the past few years."[7]

2

Practicing Biography

Lloyd Alexander did not turn to writing children's biography because he felt an urgent desire to become a biographer. The change happened quite accidentally. His agent called to tell him that Farrar, Straus and Cudahy wanted to do a series of biographies in cooperation with the scholarly Jewish Publication Society and suggested that since the offices of the Jewish Publication Society were in Philadelphia Alexander might want to make an appointment with them and talk about their plans.

Alexander decided to see if the project might interest him and arranged to meet with the Society's editor, Solomon Grayzel. Grayzel was a scholarly rabbi with a good sense of humor, and Alexander immediately felt comfortable with him. His only qualm was his lack of knowledge about the Jewish faith since he was not Jewish. Grayzel explained that the Society hoped to do nonsectarian biographies, that they wished to depict Jewish heroes in good stories for children, but that they wanted the stories to concentrate on the personalities and their contributions to history rather than on them as Jews. He suggested that Alexander might like writing a biography about August Bondi, a Jew who had known John Brown in the Kansas days prior to the American Civil War. He lent Alexander Bondi's journal, which had been published by the Kansas Historical Society, and Alexander went home to make up his mind.

Although Alexander did not purposely choose to write biographies about early Jewish heroes, he appreciated the opportunity to express some of his beliefs by placing Jewish heroes within the framework of American history. He had been raised in a family that was not tolerant of other religions. His mother had warned him against Catholics, and Jews simply were not mentioned in his household. His attitudes changed in the military service however. He realized how senseless prejudice was and cultivated new friends. When he returned home with a French Catholic bride and her daughter, he committed himself to a new life. His World War II experiences had made him aware of the need for humanitarianism, and he wanted to show how religious tolerance was a part of America's greatness.

Also, America's Civil War history had always interested Alexander. What he knew about John Brown had piqued his curiosity earlier. After reading about Bondi, he knew he wanted to take on the project, but he realized that he would need to know more about the era, John Brown, Bondi, and the Kansas problem. For the first time in his life Alexander found that he would need to do research at the library in order to write the story he wanted to tell.

"I hated the library," he has confessed. "It was one of those government institutions that my family had taught me to stay away from when I was growing up." Still, he wanted to write the book, and so he determined to teach himself to do library research. He searched the card catalog, looked at general reference resources, asked the librarians for help, and finally even wrote to the Kansas Historical Society for further information on the Bondi family. He consulted with reference librarians at the University of Kansas and the University of Pennsylvania and used the American Jewish Archives. By the time his research was finished he had a comfortable feeling about libraries, and he has continued to consult them throughout his writing career.

Borderhawk: August Bondi

Borderhawk: August Bondi is the biography of an American Jew who immigrated to this country from Vienna after the 1848 uprising. Alexander concentrates on Bondi's activities in the Kansas struggle, weaving Bondi's and John Brown's adventures together to show how the question of slavery divided the country and caused strife.

Alexander did not write this biography for children. He still considered himself an adult novelist and he wrote the story without considering that a younger audience might require a different approach to writing. In addition, he was not writing fiction. Instead, he wrote this book in an objective style acceptable to historians.

Because Alexander had access to Bondi's journal with many day-to-day accounts, he felt no need to invent the events of Bondi's life. He added little to the plot of the story and included Bondi's thoughts as much as possible. Although the book starts with Bondi's activities in the 1848 Vienna uprising, his life in Austria is described only briefly, in order to set the stage for Bondi's move to America. Within the first eleven pages of the book, Alexander describes Bondi's involvement in the 1848 riots, his father's loss of his fortune and imprisonment, his mother's sacrifices to keep the two children and herself fed, and the family's eventual decision to move to America once Bondi's father returns home.

It is not until the second page of the second chapter that Alexander begins to develop a definite time frame, writing, "The voyage lasted forty-eight days and the impatience of the fifteen-year-old boy grew with each passing hour."[1]

In the first two chapters Alexander uses very little conversation. Instead, he recounts details of the family, telling how they settled in St. Louis after their initial arrival in New Orleans and explaining that young August Bondi held various jobs before he decided to leave St. Louis, travel to New Orleans, and join Commodore Perry's expedition to Japan. At this point, Alexander begins to build upon August Bondi's Jewish heritage and his understanding of how slavery affects a race. He creates a compassionate hero, writing, "August saw Negroes dressed in nothing but coffee sacks with holes cut out for their head and arms: among them strode a white man with a straw hat and shaggy beard, a riding whip under his arm, looking as wicked as one of

Pharaoh's overseers. August turned away, sick at heart. . . . He thought of his own people, Israel, in captivity" (*Bondi*, 18).

In the next ten pages he quickly relates how Bondi stays in America and is hired by a riverboat captain as a clerk and interpreter. When Bondi accidentally hits a black man with a rope's end and sees the trust held by the man dissolve, he realizes he can no longer live in the South, and the slave question can finally become Alexander's focal point.

Bondi never really develops into a personality who can hold the reader's interest. He seems distant, perhaps due to Alexander's decision to write an accurate, historical biography. He lacks any real faults, possibly because Alexander used Bondi's journal and Bondi never revealed his own problems.

Written in the third person, *Borderhawk: August Bondi* contains little conversation. However, Alexander's descriptions of Bondi and his activities when he moves to Kansas and fights for Kansas's entry into the union as a free state contain enough drama for the typical biography reader who wishes to read about the deeds of a famous person. This first biography meets the standards of biographical writing: all of Bondi's thoughts are documented, and the details of his life are accurate. Alexander includes a few fictionalized scenes, which lend credibility to Bondi's activities without disrupting and authenticity of the retelling. However, the descriptions of Bondi in particular scenes are as Alexander imagined him to be. These are Alexander's major means of creating a personality for Bondi.

Although Alexander could not be sure of Bondi's physical appearance, he describes him at various times in the story. For instance, during Bondi's journey from St. Louis to Kansas, Alexander begins to develop the feeling that Bondi was a man of action who would fight desperately for a cause he believed in by describing him as a man who "sat tall and straight in his saddle." He continues by describing a scene that might have happened. He says that as Bondi begins his journey to Kansas he stops his horse so that he can have one last look at St. Louis. He has, Alexander informs the reader, begun to grow a beard and he depicts Bondi wearing a wide brim slouch hat, boots that reach to his knees, and a coarse jacket. Symbolically, he carries a new Colt pistol and the old tefillin that he brought with him from Vienna (*Bondi*, 35–36). These two details bolster Alexander's image of Bondi as a religious Jew willing to fight for a cause.

Because *Borderhawk: August Bondi* is thoroughly researched and Bondi is not intentionally fictionalized, it does not reveal the literary qualities that make Alexander's writing so appealing. It lacks the vivid scenes that bring Alexander's later stories alive and does not contain the strong characterization found in his later writings.

Alexander develops two minor Jewish male characters, who also travel to Kansas, in this case to set up a store. Because they are fictional, they seem more lifelike than Bondi. Alexander uses them to demonstrate the area's prejudices against Jews as well as blacks. The two storekeepers try to stay out of the slavery argument but, finally, are forced to take sides when the mild-mannered Wiener is verbally abused. Alexander writes:

> "I've taken your insults," Wiener said, his voice deathly calm. "When you insult me as a person, it makes no difference. I pay no attention. But when you insult me as a Jew . . ."
>
> The farmer bent forward and thrust his face toward Weiner's. "And what all do you aim to do about it, Jew?"
>
> Weiner slowly took off his apron. "I'm going to throw you out." (*Bondi*, 61–62)

Although this is a book about August Bondi, a Jewish freedom fighter who risked his life for emancipation, he is not the central hero or the most complex character in the story. Rather, John Brown, who is anticipated in the narrative for thirteen pages before his arrival at the scene, is the most dramatically drawn personality. Brown is recreated for the reader in several fictionalized scenes, some involving Bondi. For instance, when August Bondi and Brown's sons meet, the purported discussion of John Brown draws a picture of a romantic hero. Alexander writes:

> "Who is the Old Man?" August asked.
>
> Jason gave a short laugh. "Who is he? Or what is he!

It ain't always easy to tell. Sometimes he's like a rock.
Sometimes he's more like an old eagle. Or a wild man
with a bible in one hand and a sword in the other. I seen
him nurse Owen through a fever, gentle as a woman. I
seen him with tears in his eyes when one of his lambs
got et up. And I seen him other ways. You wait a bit,
neighbor, you'll find out soon enough." (*Bondi*, 47–48)

Alexander carefully creates John Brown's personality and
points out what Bondi and all those around Brown must have
believed: Brown was a complex man driven almost to madness in
his resolution to end slavery. No one, not even his own sons, dared
to argue with his decisions. Alexander shows that Brown's leaving
Kansas and his subsequent death deeply affected Bondi. He says
that Bondi felt he had failed because he knew what Brown hoped
to do, knew it was impossible, but did nothing to stop him, that
he later considered Brown a martyr. When the war breaks out
and he is fighting on the Union side, Bondi has the troops sing
"The Battle Hymn of the Republic." He thinks of Brown and
muses, "The Old Man had never seemed closer; perhaps he could
hear the words" (*Bondi*, 156).

In a fictional book, that moment would be called the climax,
and in many ways it is for Bondi's story. Bondi is wounded in the
next chapter and is sent home to settle down with his wife and
child. Alexander ends his hero's story, much like a work of fiction,
with a final journey home. Bondi returns to Vienna for the fiftieth
anniversary of the 1848 uprising. An honored hero to his old
friends, Bondi tells them of his struggles in the United States
against slavery and declares, "I was born here. But this is no
longer my home. Home is the land we grow in, the places and
people we love. My home is America" (*Bondi*, 181). Alexander's
old hero returns to Kansas and dies peacefully in his declared
homeland, happy to have seen the end of slavery.

With *Borderhawk*'s publication Alexander had become a children's author. Still, he did not consider himself one. He knew little
about the world of children's publications and so was surprised to
learn that there was a special award given each year to one ex-

emplary children's book with a Jewish theme. In 1959 the Isaac Seigel Memorial Juvenile Award was presented to *Borderhawk: August Bondi.* Alexander was asked to come to New York City and accept his award. Feeling honored, he went unaware that he would have to deliver an acceptance speech. That first award winner's speech was given "off the cuff." Since then, Alexander has written acceptance speeches.

The Flagship Hope: Aaron Lopez

The Jewish Publication Society's Grayzel suggested that Alexander might want to do another biography about someone who had lived during another time period, and he gave Alexander information on several Jewish heroes. One of them, Aaron Lopez, captured Alexander's imagination.

Lopez came from the Marrano community in Lisbon to the United States and was active in the movement for independence during the American Revolutionary War. Having lived in Philadelphia for most of his life surrounded by reminders of the history of the Revolutionary War, Alexander was pleased at the chance to write about an American era that had always fascinated him.

There was less information on Lopez, and that gave Alexander an opportunity to try his hand at a much more fictionalized approach to biography. He could round out his hero's personality and develop it consistently, invent conversations, and suggest how the Jewish community fit into New England during those early days of settlement in the United States. His end result, *The Flagship Hope: Aaron Lopez,* is a fine work, which opens a discussion on the literary aspects of biography and encourages an analysis of how the nonfiction element works in biographical writing.

When literary critic James L. Clifford wrote about the craft of writing literary biography, he suggested that biography had much in common with fiction. Both genres, he said, have to create a story that gives the illusion of reality by combining facts and interpretations. The problems for a biographer reside in accurately reflecting another person's attitudes. Clifford suggests that the biographer who lives in another era with a new set of values and responses may never truly discover the forces that drove his subject. And if he does, how will he make those responses clear to his modern reader?[2]

Because Alexander found little information about Lopez, he reinterpreted Lopez's life, using the real biographical information available to validate his presentation. Most of the attitudes given to Lopez within this biography are based upon authorial suppositions. Alexander did not have a journal to follow, and so he had more freedom in interpreting Lopez's actions.

Alexander chose to retell Lopez's life in story structure. Many of the street scenes, conversations, and interactions among the various personalities were created by Alexander. Some of the most dramatic moments are fashioned out of what might have been rather than on a retelling of a recorded real event. Fact and fiction are intermingled in order to present a more consistent, more readable story.

The story concentrates on Lopez's life in the United States during the American Revolution, although the action begins in Lisbon. In this book Alexander develops his characterization through highly dramatic scenes. For instance, he begins by emphasizing Aaron Lopez's initial struggle for freedom in his native land. Within the first three pages of the text Alexander has his hero being followed and spied upon, playing a game of cat and mouse with his follower, and boldly telling the informer that he is aware of what is happening. Lopez comes across as having the personality of a fictional hero. He is clever and nonchalant, has a wry sense of humor, seems to be in the midst of some sort of intrigue, and shows a flair for the dramatic.

Lopez's actions appeal to the reader. Furthermore, Alexander has constructed the story so that the reader will not immediately sense that Lopez is a member of a persecuted minority. Lopez is a positive hero, even in his physical appearance. He is, Alexander says, "a handsome young man of one-and-twenty, his long, dark hair gathered neatly at the back of his neck by a length of black ribbon. His complexion had a faint olive tone, his eyes were deep and filled with good humor."[3] Only after the reader becomes involved with the drama is he told that Lopez is a man with a secret life that could cause his death, that he is a practicing Jew in a country where the religion is forbidden.

Lopez flees his homeland because of intolerance. He has to hide his Jewishness and must affect the customs of others, even in having a non-Jewish name, Duarte. Alexander uses real events, combined with fictional scenes, to create an understanding of the psychological problems that evolve from persecution. In a stream-of-consciousness dialogue in his second chapter, he shows how religious intolerance robs the people of their own dignity. Lopez is lying in bed next to his sleeping wife and asks himself, "Who am I?" Alexander continues:

> Years ago, in childhood, the question had sometimes come to him during a sleepless night such as this, because at times Duarte saw himself as two different people. Mornings in the beautiful white house, behind locked doors, he and his father prayed together, taking the phylacteries from a hiding place at the bottom of an old chest.
>
> This was one person. And the other? As he grew older . . . Duarte met other young men from some of Lisbon's most important families. They were carefree, at ease with themselves living freely without any secrets. . . . He acquired an elegance of dress, a taste for style, he walked with the bearing of an aristocrat.
>
> . . . Yet, often, in the midst of a gay party, . . . the laughter would go out of him and he would turn away, knowing in his heart that somehow he did not belong there. (*Lopez,* 12)

Once Lopez comes to America, he is able to become a part of an active Jewish community. He takes the Hebrew name Aaron and remarries his wife in a Jewish ceremony. Thus, American tolerance is suggested.

Alexander incorporates historic realities within his fictionalized story. Lopez's life includes the strong Jewish community found in his new home, but his best friend is the historical Ezra Stiles, a Congregationalist minister with tolerant views who lived during Revolutionary War times. Stiles is not presented as a man without prejudices, however. At one point, he says that "Indians are not all peace-loving." Aaron defends the Indians, saying that they have been used by the white settlers and their governments. Then, he delivers Alexander's message, saying, "each man must have the freedom to follow his own way. Otherwise, we all suffer" (*Lopez*, 46).

And so, the idea that America has never truly been a land without prejudice is found in Alexander's retelling of Lopez's life. Aaron Lopez is slandered by two "community leaders" for being Jewish. Alexander implies that Lopez's interest in American independence stems from his need to be free from the prejudices that have inhibited him in the past when he tells his reader, "the same forces that made him cling to being a Jew, and the belief in justice and independence had already determined which way he must follow" (*Lopez*, 81).

Within his fictionalized biography Alexander has created a realistic personality. However, it is difficult to separate Lopez's values from Alexander's. It is entirely possible that Lopez's earlier experiences in Lisbon, like Alexander's experiences during World War II, caused him to become a patriot longing for independence. Still, there is nothing to ascertain that this is "true history." Lopez is imagined by Alexander to have certain values, and they are carefully placed in invented scenes. Although the attitudes are probable, they are not certain.

The author builds a story for his reader. He relates facts about a particular man whose existence has been documented in a particular time, but he also builds a drama. He uses his talents as a fiction writer to develop a scene, create a sense of danger, and maintain the reader's interest in his story. Lopez is very much a personality, and yet, he is built for the reader by the author's vision of a time and a place in history. He is, in a sense, a device manipulated by the author so that the reader can travel to another time and place.

Although this book is about Aaron Lopez, it is equally about the American colonists and their gradual need to free themselves from British rule. Alexander signals to his reader that the book is more than a biography, that it has something to say about the era by placing Lopez's name second in his title. The title implies that this is first and foremost a story about hope.

The ship *Hope* symbolizes Aaron Lopez. It stands out in a crowd and behaves differently from the other ships in the harbor. Alexander's title shows the paralleling. At the same time, Lopez is symbolic of his contemporaries. He has been documented as one of the early civic leaders who fought for justice and freedom for the Colonies, but in Alexander's book he represents the colonial sentiments of many patriots. His philosophical conversations with his friends contain the issues that were being debated by all of the colonists. By illustrating Aaron Lopez's personal story, his common hopes and frustrations, and his own goals through conversations and street scenes, Alexander brings both history and Lopez alive.

Alexander uses language to re-create another era. His use of description and dramatic scenes gives the reader a sense of the past, an interpretation of the American Revolution. Alexander's accounts of the sights and sounds of Newport, based on his research, add a sense of reality to the story that would otherwise be missing. The loss of Lopez's house during the war, his two marriages, and his status as a leading merchant are all verifiable events. Yet, the story depends upon Alexander's framing of historical events to create an interpretation of history. Alexander's perspective, in turn, has been shaped by his past.

Alexander's own experiences caused him to give prejudice and the need to struggle for personal dignity primary emphasis. Although his major anti-Semitic scene occurs in Europe, he makes it clear that oppression causes distrust and eventually uprisings. Alexander is aware that Americans were slow to join forces and begin their war efforts in both colonial times and prior to World War II, but that in the end they fought for human rights. Alexander's carefully constructed story shows the reader that the cries for freedom have not caused people to fight, that men fight for economic reasons rather than idealistic ones.

Based on historical data, this children's biography becomes a fictionalized story of an unsung American hero. Although *The Flagship Hope* did not win any awards, it is a better written book than Alexander's first, more historically accurate children's biography. It presents a clearer picture of the past, but it also reflects the attitudes that Alexander chose to emphasize.

Has Alexander stepped over the line of historical interpreter and become a reconstructionist based upon his own beliefs? Or, is his interpretation valid based upon the historical evidence available? And even if Alexander's interpretation is valid, does his injection of attitudes in creatively written dramatic scenes lessen the book's value as a children's biography? These philosophical questions make Alexander's book more meaningful. They suggest that the book is open to new interpretations, that it can facilitate a discussion on the elements found in fictionalized biography. Yet, though Alexander's second biography poses critical questions, it is not recognized as a groundbreaker in children's literature. It won no awards when it was released; today it is out of print.

Alexander had enjoyed writing biography, but after writing two he knew that he didn't want to continue pursuing the genre. He liked the fictional aspects of writing better than he did the crafting together of history and people. He had learned to do library research and has continued to use the library. However, he felt a need to write a different kind of story.

3

A New World: The Prydain Series

Alexander returned to the Celtic Arthurian lore he had read as a child and experienced as an adult while overseas during World War II when he began writing his book *Time Cat*. While he researched Celtic legend, he was drawn to the Welsh world recreated in Lady Charlotte Guest's edition of *The Mabinogion,* and he was determined to write a fantasy series. After exchanging the Welsh adventure for an Irish one in *Time Cat,* he turned his attention to the Celtic materials and began to research the legends in earnest. His research led him to conclude that Welsh mythology had been "irreparably tampered with," and so he determined his own fantasy series could be very loosely based on what he found.[1]

When she published her translations of the stories found in *The Welsh of the Llyfr Coch o Hergest* in 1877, Lady Charlotte Guest dedicated her book to her children. She wanted these stories to "cultivate" her sons' interest in Celtic legend, to instill patriotism in their hearts, and to create a "firm attachment to your Native Country."[2] Although Guest implies that she collected her stories for children, her volume will not be enjoyed by today's children because of the stilted language style and scholarly bent of her translations. Her book can be considered a reference source to the early derivations of Arthurian lore.

Creating New Legends from Old

In his "Author's Note" for *The Book of Three,* Alexander suggests that he has written his books for instructive purposes also. His goals, however, reflect his twentieth-century background and imply that his stories belong to all children who question their existence, no matter their nationality. Alexander tells his reader, "Most of us are called on to perform tasks far beyond what we can do. Our capabilities seldom match our aspirations, and we are often woefully unprepared. To this extent, we are all Assistant Pig-Keepers at heart."

While Lloyd Alexander's Prydain books are based upon his studies of Celtic mythology, they do not retell the past legends. Alexander wrote his series for the contemporary child. Aware that Celtic lore is not considered mythic by modern children, he did not set out to give children the authentic legends. What he liked about the legends he kept intact. What he didn't, he left out. His tales contain remnants from Celtic mythology while emphasizing new ideas and characters that meet the needs of young modern readers. His episodes contain heroes the preteen reader can identify with, plots with enough adventure to entice his audience into "the ancient land of Prydain," and resolutions that fulfill the dictates of fantasy in children's literature.

The adult heroes who are drawn from the legends are not the focus in Alexander's books. One of Alexander's adults, Gwydion is depicted as a war lord, a leader in battle. Lady Guest's Gwydion is described as, "the double character of poor and poet" who used those extraordinary powers in battle. His powers as enchanter, we are told, were taught to him by Math.[3] Another adult character, Alexander's Dallben, seems to be fashioned after Math who, Lady Guest says, "would seem to have excelled all the enchanters of Welsh fiction (except, perhaps, the mighty Merlin and his own pupil, Gwydion)" (*Mabinogion,* 434). Alexander's Dallben is the typical good wizard who can see into the future, and he knows Taran's heritage. Yet, though his knowledge is mentioned in the story, Dallben never captures the reader's attention. He is too distant and perfect. Gwydion, the "real" legendary hero from *The Mabinogion,* remains an exemplary character who, while not entirely devoid of faults, is past his need for typical adolescent self-doubts. His actions are already driven by altruistic goals. He does not seek glory for himself; he hopes to save his country and his people from destruction. Lady Guest mentions Dallben in her notes on *Kilhwch and Olwen* and says that he owned a magical pig named Henwen (*Mabinogion,* 268–69). Alexander took that concept and created the pig Hew Wen, who is central to the action in Alexander's first book. Although the adult heroes were the central characters in the Welsh legends, they are not Alexander's.

When Alexander wrote his series, the Celtic legends in *The Mabinogion* were unknown to American children. The heroes in the original stories are adults, struggling with adult concerns and desires. In his cycle, Alexander creates a youthful male hero to give the story new life. None of these adult characters is as realistically defined as the young people in Alexander's Prydain books. The change in focus from the adult superhero to the immature teen causes the tales to lose some of their mythic wonder, much the same way that C. S. Lewis's series softens Christian doctrine for youthful audiences. In both cases, the authors move the focus of their stories away from the absolutes of a religion. They present prevalent moral issues concerning honor, loyalty, trust, and courage. Alexander's series shows his contemporary reader that though the hero's fate is shaped by events, his decisions are his own. Thus, Alexander has suggested the outcome of events depends upon the integrity of the hero.

The Book of Three

In his introduction to *The Book of Three,* the first of a five-volume series, Alexander tells his reader that the book is loosely based upon Welsh mythology and explains that most of the adult characters can be found in the legends. He goes on to say, "Taran the Assistant Pig-Keeper, like Eilonwy of the red-gold hair, was born in my own Prydain" (*Three,* 5). Alexander's young hero, Taran, with his self-doubts, has more in common with Alexander's youthful audience. He must learn to think less about himself and his destiny and more about the welfare of others. He must change his egocentric goals for ones that give consideration to the needs of others. He must learn that sometimes a hero must let others win the hero's praise in order for the right cause to prevail.

The Book of Three concerns Taran's need to become a hero, to discover who he is, and to return home content with himself. Alexander's plot revolves around Taran's journey from his safe home into the dangerous woods where he meets and is joined by youthful companions who also are struggling towards self-realization. The book fulfills the typical structural demands of the circular journey, and it reads like earlier Arthurian adventure stories. However, Taran's adventures in the first book of the series create a concerned youth, not an adult hero. He ends his adventures with youthful attitudes that must be reckoned with on later journeys.

Within *The Book of Three*, Alexander uses typical fantasy structural and symbolic devices and stereotypic characters to create a conventional fantasy world. He incorporates devices that will appeal to youthful readers. Taran follows the male's questing heroic pattern of home-away-home. He encounters an evil enchantress and a lord of darkness. The story contains an all-knowing wizard. There are three traveling companions in the adventure—Taran, Eilonwy, and Fflewddur Fflam—and a fourth character—Gurgi—a half-man, half beast who acts as faithful servant. Taran and Eilonwy are the central protagonists of the story. Fflewddur Fflam, the young harper who is making his living as a minstrel, continuously steps between Taran and Eilonwy to save them from misunderstanding one another. Since he is older and wiser than the other two from the beginning, he changes less than they do. His journey is not a bildungsroman one. He is simply an adventurer, a troubadour who travels along to see the sights, helps when he can, and gathers tales for his job as a wandering bard.

Magic comes into play. Taran first sets out on his adventure when Hen Wen, the oracular pig, escapes from Dallben's farm. Taran and Eilonwy retrieve an ancient sword with rubric writing on it from a king's barrow. Fflewddur Fflam's harp strings break if he overembellishes his stories. Prydain's future is outlined in Dallben's magical volume, also called *The Book of Three*. Since magic is common in fantasy literature, these details add credibility to the story's structure.

Thus, *The Book of Three* is more traditionally structured than later portions of the series. This helps to set a framework for the multivolumed presentation. In *The Book of Three* the geography of Prydain is introduced while the champions travel. The book also contains a traditional map of the terrain, a common device used by fantasy authors. Prydain becomes a familiar country for the reader by the end of this book. The three central youthful protagonists who will continue to link the books seem representative of the traditional trio found in children's literature. Throughout the first book the three characters act in ways that should seem plausible to the audience. The hero is searching for heroism; the heroine seeks adventure and escape from the confines of castle life. The harper is wandering about the countryside and gaining experience so that he can become a bard.

Other characters are representative of the conflict between good and evil. Gwydion, the older war lord, is taking on the traditional role of the Arthurian leader who inspires his men to battle. The old enchanter Dallben, with his book that foretells the future, acts as the warning voice in the drama, but he is unable to stop the warlike conflicts with his knowledge. Only action and a display of courage from the three youths can stop the evil forces from overtaking Prydain.

Although the two youthful characters and the beast-man Gurgi are Alexander's inventions, they fit within the established pattern of children's fantasy literature. They resemble the heroes in the earlier Arthurian fantasy written by British authors C. S. Lewis and T. H. White. They let the reader assume she knows what to expect.

Taran and Eilonwy are orphans, a common circumstance in children's literature. However, Eilonwy knows what she is to be when she grows up, while Taran has no inkling. *The Book of Three* opens with Taran's desire to be more than an assistant pig-keeper. He is angry because he does not know his heritage, and he longs to know what the future holds for him. Fate has a way of handling his problems: he is drawn into the woods when Hen Wen flees during a time of danger; he travels with Gwydion until they are captured by Achren, the evil enchantress; he and Eilonwy are thrown together to renew the hunt for Hen Wen and for a sign of the country's future when they escape Achren's castle at the very moment of its destruction. Taran becomes a young hero by chance, and once he is one he learns that heroism is never easy.

Alexander's female protagonist, Eilonwy, knows her destiny. Like many adolescents, she wishes to exchange her fate for one that is more adventurous. When she first meets Taran she tells him, "My parents died and my kinsmen sent me here so Achren could teach me to be an enchantress. It's family tradition, don't you see? The boys are war leaders, and the girls are enchantresses" (*Three*, 70). In the next moment she adds that she wishes she were somewhere else, that she hates Achren, that she is not pleased with the constraints of the social system. Throughout the series she complains about wearing a crown, accepting womanly ways, and being ruled by the men in charge. She, like many of Alexander's readers, is seeking female independence from her inherited role in society.

The third central character, Fflewddur Fflam, is the only one of the three who has been fleshed from *The Mabinogion*. Of him, Guest writes, "he is ranked as one of the three sovereigns of Arthur's court who preferred remaining with him as knights, although they had territories and domains of their own" (*Guest*, 266). Alexander's Fflewddur Fflam is a contemporary version of Guest's character. He is not worried about his birthright; he has given up his kingdom in exchange for the freedom to wander throughout Prydain. As a youthful traveler who seeks adventure, he becomes the companion of the others. Alexander's Fflam does have faults and aspirations, and he has trouble controlling his imagination. He wants to change things by dreams rather than deeds, and so he imagines his deeds and those of his friends to be larger than they are. Like many adolescents, he needs to learn the differences between boasting, lying, and reporting.

Alexander creates realistic characters by exposing their foibles through conversation. The two central young heroes continually taunt each other. Their egoism is obvious throughout the first half of the book. Even when they accept the fact that they must help one another they seem at odds. Although they are likable youngsters, they are prone to typical adolescent behavior: they want everyone to listen to them while failing to hear each other out; they have verbal tantrums, accusing the others of misunderstanding them; they throw petty insults at one another; they want to lead; they don't feel appreciated by the others. In one instant they are self-assured, in the next they are full of self-doubts.

Alexander also fills the book with action that indirectly portrays the characters' attitudes. He draws the reader into the adventure by creating typical adolescent feelings of frustration. *The Book of Three* begins with a scene showing Taran in an outburst of anger. He wants to make a sword, but Coll, the farmer who supervises Taran's day-to-day routine, has asked him to make horseshoes. Alexander writes:

> Taran's arms ached, soot blackened his face. At last he dropped the hammer and turned to Coll, who was watching him critically.
> "Why?" Taran cried. "Why must it be horseshoes? As if we had any horses!" (*Three*, 9)

Coll tells Taran that his horseshoes aren't fit for horses to wear, and Taran retorts that he could make a sword. Before Coll can reply, he "snatched the tongs, flung a strip of red-hot iron to the anvil, and began hammering away as fast as he could" (*Three*, 9). The youthful reader soon learns that Taran fails at his sword making and sees Taran's disappointment as he stares at his efforts "in dismay" (*Three*, 10). Thus, Alexander draws his reader into the fantasy kingdom by creating realistic situations.

Within his drama Alexander addresses several adolescent misconceptions. He portrays the youthful need to discover meaning for oneself. The older heroes have much to share, but the young protagonists want to discover the realities of the world on their own. His adult heroes deliver sermons to their young companions much like adults do in the real world. And, like youngsters in the real world, the youths learn through experience that those lessons are true.

To illustrate that one should not always judge by appearances Alexander purposely breaks with traditional Arthurian images throughout the story. We learn that Taran has heard tales of Gwydion, the great war lord, and he has imagined him to be outwardly glorious. However, Gwydion is an ordinary looking middle-age man dressed in a "coarse and travel-stained" cloak. Taran's disappointment in the real man is obvious to both the reader and Gwydion. When Gwydion sees Taran's disdain for his ordinary appearance, he delivers his (and Alexander's) message to Taran and the reader alike, saying, "It is not the trappings that make the prince, . . . nor, indeed, the sword that makes the warrior" (*Three*, 25). A few pages later Alexander writes of Taran's growing admiration for the warrior's skills. By the end of the first fifty pages the reader is learning that things are not always what they seem.

Alexander breaks down the idea that beauty equates with goodness by having the female villain Achren appeal to Taran through her outward beauty and gestures of sympathy. Warned of her deceptiveness by Gwydion, Taran is stunned. Alexander writes, "For an instant he could not believe such beauty concealed the evil of which he had been warned. Had Gwydion mistaken her? Nevertheless, he shut his lips tightly" (*Three*, 60).

Later, as the leader of the companions, Taran learns that a hero must think of the welfare of others when he makes decisions and is reminded that others should not be judged on appearances alone. Gurgi has not been a welcome companion to Taran. His animalistic need for food and his constant whimpering irritate Taran, but when he is injured while scouring up food for a party, Taran looks at the shaggy beast with new eyes. He realizes that Gurgi is a part of their expedition and that as leader he must protect him, but he understands that his decision to help Gurgi puts the remainder of the party in jeopardy. Gurgi also understands that Taran's decision has put everyone in danger, and he trics to give the others his food. Taran becomes compassionate and tells the furry beast, "Your gift is generous . . . but you travel as one of us and you will need all your strength. Keep your share; it is yours by right; and you have more than earned it" (*Three,* 126). When Taran accepts Gurgi, he finds that Gurgi's "wet wolfhound odor" is no longer objectionable. Once again, Alexander has his hero change his subjective judgment with experience.

The meaning of heroism is central to the adventure, as Alexander suggests in his "Author's Note." He purposely shapes traditional literary images and plot patterns to emphasize that the value of an individual cannot be determined by appearance or birthright alone. In the end, Taran must learn to appreciate his role as Assistant Pig-Keeper. After he tells Dallben that he is not a hero because he was unable to perform any miraculous feat, Dallben asks him, "Does it truly matter . . . which of you did what, since all shared the same goal and the same danger? Nothing we do is ever done entirely alone" (*Three,* 223).

Alexander builds Taran's strengths throughout *The Book of Three*. During *The Book of Three* the youthful hero's courage and valor have been depicted in a traditional bildungsroman. In *The Book of Three* Alexander uses Taran's journey to show how compassion towards others builds a sense of honor. At last, when Taran saves a young gwythaint, a bird that spies on the enemies of the Lord of Darkness, and it in turn helps the companions, he learns to trust his judgments based on sympathy and understanding rather than outward appearances, and he learns to consider the results of his decisions beforehand. By the end of the book Taran has become more thoughtful and concerned for the welfare of those around him.

Because Alexander is establishing the intellectual and emotional link between Eilonwy and Taran within this first book, he introduces his female protagonist, a young princess and a talkative teen, in a scene reminiscent of the princess's encounter with the frog in the Grimm folktale "The Frog Prince." Eilonwy has lost her magic bauble, and she asks Taran to return it to her. When he calls her a little girl she bristles and responds, "Are you slow-witted? I'm sorry for you. It's terrible to be dull and stupid" (*Three,* 65). When he tells her that he is an Assistant Pig-Keeper, Eilonwy says his occupation seems "fascinating." However, his ego has no time to mend from her earlier judgment that he is stupid because in no time his lack of understanding makes her say, "I don't want to hurt your feelings by asking, but is Assistant Pig-Keeper the kind of work that calls for a great deal of intelligence?" (*Three,* 66). Eilonwy causes Taran to evaluate his intelligence, compassion, and leadership abilities. At first, she seems to be a stereotypical female teen: pretty, headstrong, and outspoken. She confuses Taran with her remarks, and he seems constantly at a loss to explain his decisions to her. When she questions his abilities, he snaps back at her with his justification for his behavior. However, she makes Taran consider the consequences of his decisions. As he listens to Eilonwy and tries to please her, Taran learns that he should think before he acts. Throughout *The Book of Three* Eilonwy and Taran maintain a healthy banter that suggests mutual respect for the other person's opinions.

The girl is portrayed as a positive character from the start, but she is not seen by Taran at first. When he finally sees Eilonwy, he discovers that she is quite attractive. She has long flowing reddish gold hair, delicate features, and high cheekbones. Alexander writes, "She was one or two years younger than he, but fully as tall" (*Three,* 69). Thus, Alexander establishes Eilonwy as Taran's physical equal. Furthermore, his earlier use of conversation has established that she is not a typical medieval princess to be worshiped from afar. She is argumentative and judgmental, just as Taran is. Although she is attractive, it is not her looks which Taran finds interesting. He continually reacts to her behavior and her remarks more than her looks.

At times Taran must depend upon Eilonwy. She frees him from Achren's castle, and she brings the sword from the barrow. She is the one who decides that the companions must all travel together, and her magic saves them from the evil Cauldron-Born warriors. She is an active, thinking heroine capable of doing heroic deeds. In the end, she is an equal to Taran. As the book closes, Taran tells Eilonwy that she will remain with him at Caer Dallben and is told, "I suppose . . . it never occurred to you to *ask* me. . . . You usually don't" (*Three*, 224).

Alexander's male and female protagonists maintain a sense of romantic conflict throughout much of the book. Because the evil forces can be seen only from afar, there needs to be another complication while the young people travel through their adventures. This love/hate relationship is typical of many adolescents. Like most early teens, these two cannot decide whether they want to agree or disagree. The bantering that continues to the very end of the story suggests that the book's end is not a final resolution to their conflict of wills. It establishes a need for another volume and suggests that the two still lack sympathy for each other. Part of their unresolved relationship rests on the fact that Taran's personality is still immature, and part rests on Eilonwy's critical nature.

The reader understands that this is the beginning of a series when he reaches the end of *The Book of Three*. Alexander has not resolved the conflict between Taran and Eilonwy. And, Taran has not become a real hero. Gwydion tells him, "You are still as touchy and headstrong as ever. . . . The dreams of heroism, of worth, of achievement are noble ones; but you, not I, must make them come true" (*Three*, 219). Dallben reminds him that on his first adventure he has been impetuous, full of self-pity, and a dreamer, and the reader senses that it will take at least one more journey to make him a hero.

This first book has established the main characters of Alexander's saga; because Alexander has carefully developed his young protagonists, they have become realistic personalities. Youthful readers look for the remaining books because they are intrigued with the building relationship between Taran and Eilonwy, interested in learning how Fflewddur Fflam and Gurgi fare in the end, and want to see the end of the struggle against evil.

The adult heroes are still the guiding forces when *The Book of Three* ends. The youthful reader, inexperienced in the world's ways will find this satisfying, but will look forward to the day when Taran is a hero in his own right. Thus, using the most common motifs of fantasy, Alexander has created a feeling of modernism by creating youthful characters to maintain his readership.

When Alexander discussed his writing in 1966, he called the elements of the Welsh tales in his stories "threads from broader fantasies" that had to be woven together in his new story. Concerning the use of ancient legends, he said, "Writers have drawn on them for centuries without exhausting them."[4]

The Black Cauldron

In his second book, *The Black Cauldron,* Alexander again uses elements from Welsh legend. The cauldron had been mentioned in Guest's notes for her translation of "Branwen the Daughter of Llyr" as a wicked pot brought into the land by invaders. It could change fallen warriors into animated corpses, called the Cauldron-Born, who would fight against their comrades. Alexander used the Caldron-Born in his first book, and he makes the pot and its evil ways the focal point in his second adventure. *The Mabinogion* also tells of a man stronger than all others who travels across the country carrying the pot on his back. In Alexander's version, the young companions capture the pot only to have it taken from them by a prince who resembles the legendary man in his strength and determination and who wants glory at all costs. A second new young hero based on Lady Guest's *Mabinogion* is introduced. The ancient Adaon is a bard celebrated for his valor. In the end, Guest explains, he was assassinated, but even after death he is said to have avenged his enemy (*Guest,* 325). Eilonwy is also in Lady Guest's book as the heroine Branwen, who teaches her pet crow to speak. The talking starling appears in *The Black Cauldron* and helps the companions, but it is not Eilonwy's bird. Alexander does call the bird Kaw, the surname of a branch of Arthur's relatives in *The Mabinogion.* He ties these details into his own story, *The Black Cauldron.*

However, this second book is not a simple retelling of Welsh legend. As a part of a series designed for twentieth-century readers, it contains the problems of today's youth. *The Black Cauldron* is the realistic depiction of Taran's growth from a strong-willed and self-centered youth to a thoughtful leader. And, it develops the continual shift in Taran's relationship with Eilonwy. Thus, although this book relies heavily on the plot and symbols found in ancient Celtic lore, the old elements are restructured to fit Alexander's needs. The story is appealing to modern young readers because it depicts young people as the central characters engaged in captivating adventures. Alexander tells the readers of *The Black Cauldron,* "Although an imaginary world, Prydain is essentially not too different from our real one, where humor and heartbreak, joy and sadness are closely interwoven. The choices and decisions that face a frequently baffled Assistant Pig-Keeper are no easier than the ones we ourselves make. Even in a fantasy realm, growing up is accomplished not without cost."[5] The reader is also warned that the adventure in this second volume contains "a darker thread" than the one in the first book. The book's audience will see death and destruction before the end of this journey.

Alexander casts a foreboding atmosphere in his setting. It is autumn when the book opens, and Alexander paints a dismal scene, saying, "Many trees were already leafless, and among the branches clung the ragged edges of the empty nests" (*Cauldron,* 1). The first two paragraphs concentrate upon the weather, and the entire scene seems bleak. When Prince Ellidyr arrives on horseback, he is described as little better than the weather. He has black eyes that are deeply set in an arrogant face. His clothes are old and worn, though they have been painstakingly patched. Even his horse is unattractive, with an expression "as ill-tempered as her master's" (*Cauldron,* 2). There is no suggestion of optimism, and little reason to believe that Taran will have the same sort of adventure he had in *The Book of Three.*

Immediately, Alexander uses a series of physical descriptions, conversations, and action to draw his reader into the story's central conflict between the adolescent protagonist (Taran) and the adolescent antagonist (Ellidyr). The country's turmoil, caused by the struggle of good against evil, will be introduced later, but here the book centers on the struggle between Taran and Ellidyr.

Within the first chapter, the reader learns that, though Ellidyr has a title and unusual strength, he has nothing else. As the youngest son, he has not inherited land or an estate. Yet, Ellidyr has become a bully and a snob. He feels that he should be looked up to by the others, and he wants to establish his place as the leader of the companions once they begin their journey. Taran dislikes Ellidyr and resents Ellidyr's attempts to lead the companions. He wants to be acknowledged as Ellidyr's equal. Both Ellidyr and Taran are acting like rival teenagers who want to control the others and win their respect at the same time. The two young men are at conflict because neither feels that his needs are being met. Both seek to be heroes.

Although Ellidyr is depicted as the more spiteful and self-centered of the two, Taran is equally headstrong for the first third of the book. He fights back and insults Ellidyr at every turn. Taran's personal quest for importance reflects a common adolescent concern.

Adaon is the true hero in the first third of the book. Able to foresee the future, he chides Ellidyr for his short temper and his behavior. At one point he says, "Is there not glory enough in living the days given to us? You should know there is adventure in simply being among those we love and the things we love, and beauty too" (*Cauldron,* 92). Like Guest's hero in *The Mabinogion,* Adaon is destined to die. Alexander forewarns the reader in chapter 3 of his death. When Adaon is killed, Taran loses his childish ways and begins to think differently. Adaon's death allows Taran to become the leader and the story's hero. Yet, even after his death Adaon's powers first save the group's companions. Prior to his last battle, he tells Taran that if he falls in battle Taran should take his packet of healing herbs, his horse, and a brooch given to him by his betrothed. The brooch carries magical powers; it conjures visions of the future and leads the companions on their journey.

Later in the book Taran has visions and is forced to consider the magical powers of Adaon's brooch. When he discusses it with Eilonwy and Fflewddur Fflam, Eilonwy replies, "Adaon's clasp is a priceless gift. It gives you a kind of wisdom . . . which, I suppose, is what Assistant Pig-Keepers need more than anything else"

(*Cauldron*, 109). Through Eilonwy, Alexander tells his audience that two of the chief ingredients of heroism are the ability to perceive what should be done and the intelligence to carry it out. These are the traits Taran will have by the end of the book.

As the group's leader, Taran is forced to choose between keeping the brooch and his newly acquired wisdom and freeing the cauldron from the clutches of the three swamp witches, Orddu, Orgoch, and Orwen. Because he feels the witches might misuse the cauldron, he gives up his powers, sacrificing his gains for the sake of the kingdom and becoming a hero. He gives up his dependence on magic and learns to depend upon his own strength and courage.

Ellidyr deserts the companions to look for the cauldron on his own prior to Adaon's death. Yet, because Alexander has carefully developed the conflict between Taran and Ellidyr, the reader knows that Ellidyr will reappear. When he does, the heroes have rescued the cauldron and are returning to the adults. Taran tells Ellidyr that the cauldron can be destroyed only if a man sacrifices himself to it, and Ellidyr replies, "Why not climb in it yourself? Surely you are bold enough. Or are you a coward at heart, when the test is put to you?" (*Cauldron*, 186). Alexander is using self-prophecy. It is a broken Ellidyr who finally makes the sacrifice and walks willingly into the pot. When he does, he sacrifices his life to save Taran and the companions.

Although Ellidyr becomes a hero, he is not the sort of hero Alexander wants his reader to emulate. Ellidyr displays the heroism of a soldier who sacrifices everything for the cause, who takes the final order and does what he must. Statues are built for these heroes, but it is not the heroism that Alexander wishes to honor.

Taran sacrifices the supernatural in order to rely on his intuition. At the end of *The Black Cauldron* Gwydion tells Taran, "You chose to be a hero not through enchantment but through your own manhood. And since you have chosen, for good or ill, you must take the risks of a man. You may win or you may lose. Time will tell" (*Cauldron*, 228). Thus, to be heroic is to be concerned for the safety of others, forget prideful dreams, and concentrate on realistic goals.

Different types of heroism are depicted through the actions of the three young adventurers. Adaon, the noble hero, foresees his death, but he does not refuse to lead the others. He is a tragic hero. Ellidyr sacrifices his life rather than die in dishonor. He, too, ends in tragedy. In the end, only Taran returns home. His heroism has not come through fighting but through his thoughtful dealings with others.

Alexander reminds the reader that the three young men journeyed out in the fall, and now Taran is returning home to a garden that still needs to be readied for winter. Once again, the youthful Taran and his companions return home without completing their journeys. Gwydion tells the reader that Taran is not yet a man. His relationship with Eilonwy is less frenzied, but it is not resolved. A third book is needed.

The Castle of Llyr

In *The Castle of Llyr,* the third book, Alexander still uses devices from the earlier mythology. A youthful hero named Prince Rhun, a prince mentioned in Lady Guest's book, is introduced. Eilonwy is sent on a sailing venture to stay in the land of her future husband; Branwen, the model for Eilonwy, also traveled over the seas to be married in the story "Branwen the Daughter of Llyr." Like Branwen, Eilonwy's trip nearly destroys her, although for different reasons. She is not rudely treated by her prospective husband as Branwen was but is the center of an evil plot concocted by Achren, her sinister aunt from *The Book of Three.* The story also contains Gwydion in disguise as a cobbler, a central scene of deception in the legend "Manawyddan the Son of Llyr."

However, for all the similarities, the story marks a break with the earlier Welsh material. *The Castle of Llyr* is a romantic novel that focuses on Taran's growing love for Princess Eilonwy and his frustration with the disparity between their stations in life. Alexander says in his "Author's Note" that Taran is aware of his feelings and that his situation makes the story bittersweet rather than heroic.[6] Most of the story involves the efforts of Taran, Prince Rhun, Fflewddur Fflam, and Gurgi to save Eilonwy from her aunt. Now, however, Rhun, in his eagerness to do heroic deeds and be noticed, resembles Taran in *The Book of Three,* while Taran, who is level-headed and self-sacrificing, acts like Gwydion.

The story involves a love triangle, and it signals Taran's manhood. Throughout the book the reader is made aware of Taran's strong feelings for Eilonwy. Yet the legendary princess has been sent abroad to meet her future husband. Since the tale revolves around Taran's growing awareness of his love for Eilonwy, it cannot focus on the legends. Taran is outside of the original material. Once it is clear that Taran, not Rhun, is Eilonwy's favorite, the story breaks with Celtic legend, and the reader senses the newness of Alexander's story. Since Prydain is firmly established for the series reader and the fantasy seems realistic, the legendary elements can become secondary to the human drama.

Taran's heroism in the first three books depends upon his perception of ensuing danger. In each of the books Taran refuses to listen to his companions' suggestion that they return and seek help. Always, Taran stresses the danger of wasting time. His adventures start when he decides to travel on without consulting others. In the first two books he purposely starts on a quest when he believes he can stop the destruction of Pyrdain. In *The Castle of Llyr,* Taran strays from the others while he is searching for Prince Rhun. In this case, his journey leads him away from the search for Eilonwy, his more immediate concern, and sets him on an aimless course. As he travels, Taran must face the realities of his ancestry.

Alexander creates a moral dilemma for Taran in *The Castle of Llyr.* He forces him to recognize that in a monarchical society he can never be Eilonwy's husband. Once Taran finds Rhun, the prince who could marry a princess, Taran admonishes him for getting lost. When Rhun replies that he cannot be lost since he is the leader of the scouting expedition, Taran replies, "Yes, you command, . . . as you were born to, as a king's son." Then he checks his anger and tells Prince Rhun, "But for your own safety, I urge you to stay close to us" (*Llyr,* 72).

Taran's role as the group's leader is an uncomfortable one; in seeking Eilonwy he seems to be assuring the end of his personal dreams. His position has reversed from the acknowledged hero to the scout, and the prince explains that he wants to be the one to save Eilonwy since she is to be his wife. Alexander shows the reader Taran's anguish when he writes, "'Eilonwy's safe return is all that matters now,' Taran began. He spoke slowly, knowing in his heart that he, no less than Rhun, yearned to be Eilonwy's rescuer. But he realized there was a decision he must face without flinching. 'The searchers by this time are far distant,' Taran said, each word costing him an effort, yet each word forcing him to a choice as painful as it was clear. . . . 'We have only one path to follow: the one back to Dinas Rhydnant'" (*Llyr*, 88–89). In the past Taran has insisted on moving forward. This time it is Rhun who insists that they not turn back, that he be allowed to find Eilonwy. By the time fate steps in and forces the companions to continue their search for Eilonwy, Rhun has accepted Taran as the real leader, but he is still seeking glory for himself to impress Eilonwy. Throughout the adventure, Taran realizes that being the group's leader will not make him Eilonwy's hero. His concern for her safety is balanced with the realization that once found and safely returned to Prince Rhun's castle she will be lost to him.

Alexander's adventure has little to do with medieval romanticism. Since this is children's literature, Eilonwy cannot marry Rhun and then have a clandestine affair with Taran in the next book. Thus, the modern reader is forced to face the fact that Taran cannot marry a princess if Alexander follows the dictates of Arthurian legend. The only hope that the reader sustains is that Alexander, as a twentieth-century writer, will break with literary patterns and create a new ending for the romantic trio.

And he does. In the last scene Taran confronts Eilonwy with the plan for her marriage to Rhun, and she angrily replies, "There's limits to having people make up your mind for you," and then she looks at Taran and continues, "Did you seriously think for a moment I would ever? . . . Taran of Caer Dallben, . . . I'm not speaking to you! At least . . . not for a little while" (*Llyr*, 205–6).

The Castle of Llyr is the shortest book in the series, yet it is extremely important because it marks the series' turning point.

From this book on, this is an American fantasy series, not a re-telling of Celtic legend. After reading *The Castle of Llyr,* the reader understands that Alexander is telling an American hero story and that he is not using the Celtic materials in traditional ways. They are remnants from a closet used to dress up a modern play. They add a distinctive quality to the story, but they do not support conventional interpretations.

Taran Wanderer

The fourth book, *Taran Wanderer,* is the beginning of a new heroic adventure which relies upon the reader's understanding of the previous books. Taran's quest to discover himself is spurred by his growing frustration about his relationship with Eilonwy. If Taran is simply an extension of earlier legends, he cannot marry a princess unless his parents are from the nobility, and he must find a royal beginning. If Taran reflects the concerns of Americans in the 1960s, his journey must be viewed as the then-popular quest to "find oneself." Taran's adventures have little to do with saving the country; instead, they are centered on Taran's own need to understand his heritage.

The first chapter "Who Am I?" sets up Taran's adventures. When the enchanter Dallben tells Taran that he does not know who Taran's parents were, Taran asks to travel in search of his past. He explains, "When Eilonwy returns, it—it is in my heart to ask her to wed. But this I cannot do, . . . this I will not do until I learn who I am."[7] As the readers may have suspected, the cycle does contain a traditional love story. However, by the end of the book Alexander will confirm that Taran is not a traditional Arthurian hero. He will not find the royal heritage needed to become a king.

Alexander assumes that his audience has read about Taran's other journeys, and he refers to the characters and symbols used earlier. He expects readers to understand the magic encountered and the seriousness of traveling through the Marshes and asking the three witches advice.

The witches tell Taran that he must find out who he is for himself, and they suggest that he travel over the Llawgadarn Mountains and consult The Mirror of Llunet. At the end of the chapter Taran begins the story's real journey.

This time, Alexander has set up a fairy-tale motif: a young hero goes out to seek adventure in order to win the hand of a young princess; he meets an old hag (in this case three) and accepts suggestions for his quest; he travels toward a magical mirror, which can reflect his past and, in turn, secure his future.

While at the witches' cottage, Taran glimpses a strange tapestry that the three enchantresses are weaving. It will reappear in the final book, but is not explained in this adventure. In the end, it turns out to be a depiction of Taran's life story. Thus, Alexander is weaving his cycle together with details that allude to past and future events.

The first half of *Taran Wanderer* contains a series of adventures that are each complete in themselves. They cajole Alexander's reader into believing that Taran's adventures will be predictable. Taran somehow stumbles onto most of his old companions from the earlier books. Because Alexander assumes the reader is familiar with these characters, he does not fully develop them. They act in predictable ways and reflect the past adventures. Taran and the reader know what to expect from these personalities. The change from familiar to new characters does not come until the reader has comfortably settled into the story.

The break with the familiar is signaled in chapter 11's title. Alexander calls the chapter "Dorath," emphasizing that a new character is arriving, that the story is shifting. Dorath is Taran's own enemy. Unlike the dark forces or the supernatural villains met earlier, Dorath is a real scoundrel. A highwayman and a thief, this man has no special powers, but he inflicts pain on others for his own pleasure. His acts against humanity will cause Taran to act in heroic ways. His meanness toward others is in direct contrast with Taran's now noble personality. Taran's adventures hit a turning point when he first confronts Dorath and is beaten by him. Once robbed of his sword, Taran looks up and asks, "What have you gained worth more to you than to me?"

Dorath's answer lets the reader know that he is a cruel and thoughtless man. He replies, "The getting pleased me, swineherd. The taking pleases me all the more" (*Wanderer*, 166). From this point on Taran is compassionate to others.

The remainder of *Taran Wanderer* centers on Taran's escape to a country where the people are more humble, are more like the common laborers of America. Taran leaves the "civilized" land of kings and queens, wizards and warlords, and moves out into the land of the peasant farmer, the sheepherder, the weaver, the potter. Alexander begins to relate his hero's journey to the journey of a contemporary youngster who leaves home to discover who he might be, what he might do. In the process, he shows how Taran learns to respect the work of the country's common citizens.

At one point in the adventure Taran stands still, forced into the realization that he might be a commoner, forcing the reader to see the difference between dreams and realities. Taran never expected to find his beginnings in a lowly station, and he is not pleased. Still, Taran accepts the possibilities of his humble beginnings. He decides he will give up his quest, confessing, "A proud birthright was all that counted for me. Those who had none— even when I admired them. . . . I deemed them lesser because of it. Without knowing them, I judged them less than they were. Now I see them as true men. Noble? They are far nobler than I" (*Wanderer*, 202). He determines to continue his journey, however, because he "cannot face Dallben or Coll." And so, he sets off to the people of the Free Commots to learn about free laborers, and Alexander's reader must turn his back on hopes of a self-fulfilling fantasy.

For the next seventy pages Taran serves as apprentice to various craftsmen and women. In the end, while he admires their skills, he determines that their work is not appropriate for him. During these ramblings Taran meets the people he will lead in the final book. Alexander's shift from his unreal fantasy world into a world more like the reader's prepares the reader for the final episode. Like Taran, they are familiar with the virtues of simple folk.

When Taran turns his horse toward home, Alexander writes,

"It seemed he could hear voices calling to him. "Remember us! Remember us!" He turned once, but Merin was far behind and out of sight. From the hills a wind had risen, driving the scattered leaves before it, bearing homeward to Caer Dallben. Taran followed it" (*Wanderer,* 272). And so, as Taran's saga nears its end, Alexander leaves the reader with a mature hero who, though he is returning home to his mentors, is no longer dependent upon the praise and the wisdom of home to determine if his journey has been a successful one. His concern is not for himself and his destiny. He has worked hard with the common people and now he is ready to meet new challenges without worrying about what will follow.

The High King

In his "Author's Note" for *The High King,* the fifth book, Alexander warns the reader to expect the unexpected and that this book is the culmination of Taran's story when the hero must make his final decision. He suggests that the reader, too, will face making "this kind of choice" many times and admits that Pyrdain is more than Wales, saying, "As for Prydain itself, part Wales as it is, but more as it never was. . . . While it grew from Welsh legend, it has broadened into my attempt to make a land of fantasy relevant to a world of reality."[8]

There is no doubt that Alexander intended this book for his experienced reader. He begins with Taran's return from the last book's journey, thus linking the two books. The reader who has followed Taran throughout the series feels a sense of reunion with old friends when reading the scene describing Taran's return.

Alexander immediately affirms Taran's heroic stance. In the midst of the rejoicing Eilonwy remarks that there is something different about Taran, that "unless you told someone they'd never guess you were an Assistant Pig-Keeper" (*King,* 12). When Taran replies that he did not find what he had hoped for, Dallben suggests that he found more than he sought and gained more from it than he might understand. Thus, Taran has returned to the land of wizards, kings, and queens as a commoner and a hero. The evil forces have not been defeated, and his work is not yet complete, so the reader anticipates a final journey.

The last book is structured much like the first book of the series. Taran is at home in Caer Dallben when danger presents itself. The Cauldron-Born lead an attack against Gwydion, and the struggles begin for one last time. The powers of evil and goodness leave Caer Dallben to fight for supreme rule over all of Prydain. Taran and his companions travel a divergent road from that of Gwydion and the mightier forces, and in the end Taran reclaims the magical sword. The final victory is followed by a journey back to Caer Dallben, and the story ends where it began.

Yet, the story is different in many ways. This time Taran is a tested hero, and his role in the battles is as important as Gwydion's. Taran depends less upon magic and dreams. He leads the people of the Free Commots. The story's predicably happy ending is tempered with the realization that this brings to an end the land of Prydain for author, reader, and characters. The battles have brought death to two of the books major heroes, Coll and Rhun. And, though the dark forces have been conquered, Dallben warns that danger is not over as long as men carry hatred in their hearts. Finally, the hero must lose his enchanted land and his friends. All those magical personalities who have been essential to Taran's growing up must leave Prydain; only Taran, Eilonwy, and Hen Wen remain behind, stripped of all supernatural powers. Taran and Eilonwy have chosen to rule the Commot people without magic. They can remain behind only if they remain as mortal leaders.

And so, Alexander brings the reader out of the magical kingdom of long ago with the realization that just leaders will accept their right to rule tempered with the realization that ruling others is best accomplished in a land where the people choose their leadership. Alexander's young Taran has become a realistic personality while he learned what it means to be a hero. In addition, he has discovered much about himself as he grew toward maturity.

While the books contain the trappings of a Celtic-based fantasy series, they are more American than British. They tell of a young man's quest beyond personal goals and glory. They suggest that the best leader is not chosen by birthright but by ability. And they propose that everyone has the possibility of becoming a hero.

The Prydain Short Stories

In addition to the lengthier books, Alexander created several shorter stories about Prydain, which give background to the land. Two of the stories appeared as picture books. The remainder appeared in a volume entitled *The Foundling and Other Tales of Prydain*. In many ways they are Alexander's own *Book of Three* because they present the earlier history of Prydain.

Alexander's first two short fantasies rely on the characters from the Prydain series. Their adventures read much like fairy tales. Because these picture book stories were published after the longer series had begun, they act as character guides to two of the series' main characters, Coll and Fflewddur Fflam.

Coll and His White Pig depicts the series' caretaker of Caer Dallben as a middle-age man who must save the pig Hen Wen from the master of death Arawn's Cauldron-Born. Although Coll was once a leader, he prefers farming to warrior duties. His kindness is stressed in his adventures. Throughout his travels he helps the creatures of the forest. When he is in danger, they help him in return. Coll represents Alexander's notion that every man can be a hero. Alexander also suggests that not every man would want to be a hero. Coll journeys only when forced to protect his pig, and he returns home content to assume his daily life as a farmer. When asked if he would like to know what the future holds for him, Coll answers that he knows what the weather will bring and that he has no yearning to know if there will be other journeys forced on him. His next journey away from Caer Dallben is in *The High King* when he is killed. Once wounded, he tells Taran, "I had hoped one day to sleep in my own garden. . . . The drone of bees would have pleased me. . . . But I see the choice was not to be mine" (*King,* 177). Thus, Alexander ends Coll's adventures on the road and shows that it is best not to know what the future brings and that man cannot choose his own fate.

Alexander's hero Fflewddur Fflam carries the author's soul. He represents Alexander, though he does come from *The Mabinogion*. Fflewddur Fflam is the hero of the second picture book. In *The Truthful Harp* the reader learns how Fflam received his harp and began his journeys. Like Alexander, Fflewddur Fflam admits that he would like to make the world a better place and that he imagines a world that is more clearly defined and heroic. This book works as a preview to the series; it presents the bard when he was an untested youth. As such, it is a companion piece with the series.

While neither of these books are necessary for the series to be successful, they round out characters who might otherwise remain basically flat. Within the Prydain Chronicles, Coll and Fflam act predictably. They do not mature or change in their attitudes. The two picture books show them as more human personalities.

Lloyd Alexander's creation of Prydain had a deep effect on him. When discussing the series, he has said that the stories contained his own philosophies. Faced with a war he could not accept and a world he found full of injustices, he felt he could deal with moral issues that he felt deeply about through his Prydain adventures. He was at a loss when he finished the five books and was not ready to completely turn away from his fantasy world.

In 1973 Alexander published the last of his Prydain books, *The Foundling and Other Tales of Prydain*. This short volume contains six stories, which told of Prydain's history prior to the Chronicles. The reader of the series might be surprised by Alexander's somber tone in these stories, but they reflect Alexander's need to explain his growing concern over America's political turmoil. His belief that war is unjust is reflected in "The Sword." In this tale the main character is a ruler who has little concern for his people and who grows fearful of them. His fear drives him to vengeful acts until he becomes trapped in a war he cannot control. In the end, his attitude causes his demise. In "The Stone" Alexander shows how futile it is to wish that the clock would stand still. Once granted everlasting youth, the story's antihero cannot grow old, and the world cannot change. At last he cries out "No! No! I want no more of it. Whatever may happen, let it happen. It's better than nothing happening at all."[9] In this story Alexander suggests that, while youth is a cherished time, it must be replaced and people must die if the world is to remain new and constantly changing.

This group of stories is less successful than the five series books or the two picture books. The characters are not carefully drawn, and the reader feels a lack of action and detail, that these stories are being told to him. He cannot experience the scenes because they are not carefully drawn. To the youthful Prydain reader, these stories may seem anticlimatic. The book does have value for the critic who wishes to discuss Alexander's personal interpretation of his twentieth-century existence and his concern about the United States's future if it continued in Vietnam.

Although Alexander uses patterns, characters, and magical elements drawn from ancient legend in his Prydain books, he creates a twentieth-century drama, which explicates his belief in man's ability to care for others, to shape fate through actions, and to create a better world for future generations. His story of Taran is a modern American drama; it does not end with Taran discovering his royal parentage. In the end Taran is a hero who has arrived "just in the nick of time" and who has grown until his concern is less with winning and more with helping others. Taran's saga demonstrates that a hero must seek to put the world back together after the battles have been fought, that a hero can long to stay home and engage in commonplace activities, and that, above all, a hero must be mature enough first to consider the welfare of others before turning to personal rewards. Taran becomes a democratic hero who wishes to rule by helping, who seeks the good of all people. Like many American literary heroes, he has not inherited wealth or fame. What he achieves he achieves by learning to accept his shortcomings and to make the right decisions.

Alexander's worldwide popularity with youths indicates that

this is a modern fantasy series created for today's reader. His ability to touch the hearts of children in diverse countries suggests that the stories have found their primary audience. In the end, it must be said that Lloyd Alexander's Prydain is his own country. It holds his visions and is the unique work of a modern American author who has incorporated archaic legends into his imaginary world.

4

Cat Tales

Lloyd Alexander developed a love of cats when he and Janine first acquired a pet. In the autobiographical novel *My Five Tigers* he comments, "When Janine first suggested taking in a cat, I refused. I still preferred dogs. Cats seemed of little consequence."[1] By 1955, after owning several felines and learning to respect their intelligence, he emerged a converted cat lover. What appealed to him about cats was their independence.

Alexander's first cat book, *My Five Tigers,* was written for cat lovers rather than children. In it he comments that cats remain mysterious, that they never fully accept humans as their equals, and that it takes a good deal of work to make a cat your friend. He shows his respect for and admiration of these creatures when he asserts, "We enjoy their intelligence and grace; and we feel a strange sense of companionship and consolation in their presence. . . . Cats are like music. The reasons for their appeal can never be expressed too clearly" (*Tigers,* 117).

Alexander's earlier change from nonfiction to fantasy happened while he was helping Manhattan veterinarian Louis J. Camuti write his autobiography, *Park Avenue Vet.* Alexander coauthored the book while he was deciding what sort of writing he wanted to do. As he worked in his study, he became intrigued by his cat Solomon's seemingly magical appearances and disappearances.

He has claimed that the cat would "simply seem to be there, then be gone." Alexander began to toy with the idea of a time-travel book structured around a cat.

At the same time he met Holt, Rinehart and Winston editor Ann Durell, also a cat lover, and mentioned he had an idea for a fantasy for children, an "art form" experience to allow him to experiment with new writing techniques. Durell encouraged him to try, and he began working on *Time Cat*. Once the book was completed and accepted by Holt, Durell became his editor. All of his remaining books have been edited by Durell.

When Alexander began researching Celtic legend, he found that cats had little place in these old tales. When he created the mystical land of Prydain, he only included his huge fantasy feline Llyan. Yet it was his research for *Time Cat* that caused him to write the Prydain cycle.

Time Cat

Time Cat: The Remarkable Journeys of Jason and Gareth combines time travel, history, and legends within an episodic plot. It centers on the experiences of a young boy and his magical cat Gareth's travels to nine different places—"anywhere, any time, any country, any century."[2]

As the story begins, Jason has been sent to his bedroom for bad behavior and is sitting on the bed with his cat, wishing out loud that he had nine lives. Gareth begins to speak to Jason and explains that as a cat he does not have nine lives, but he can visit nine other places. Alexander draws upon his experiences with Solomon when he writes, "Where do you think cats go when you're looking all over and can't find them? . . . And have you ever noticed a cat suddenly appear in a room when you were sure the room was empty?" (*Time Cat*, 9).

Throughout the book, the adventures combine historical times, legendary people, and social drama. Several observations about cats and their behavior are interspersed within the stories. Gareth and Jason travel from 2700 B.C. to contemporary times, but Alexander emphasizes the earlier periods. Alexander begins his adventures in the Egyptian court of Neter-Khet, where cats are considered sacred. As a ruler, Neter-Khet expects cats to do his bidding, but he is told by Jason that cats will not be commanded, cannot be owned, and do not like loud noises.

Alexander skips from 1775 to the 1900s. The last few stories are less compelling than the earlier ones; it is almost as if Alexander has tired of his "art form" experiment and is ready to move on to something else.

Most of *Time Cat*'s episodes fit a pattern. All but one are contained in two chapters. The first chapter sets the historical scene, introduces the main characters, and foreshadows events to come in the second chapter. At the end of the first chapter, a conflict for the boy and his cat is introduced, and the chapter ends with a cliff-hanger, a device Alexander continues to use in his later books. Foreshadowing is used in the first chapter to suggest each episode's ending. The second chapter resolves the conflict and also implies that the resolution will cause change. Most of the stories deal with the problems of poor leadership, a topic Alexander treats in his later children's books. In these first fantasies, characters change their attitudes when they learn how to deal with their cats. They give up a part of their autocratic attitudes as they discover the need to be concerned about the feelings and conditions of others. For example, in the Japanese episode, the young emperor learns to make decisions that help his subjects, while in the story set on the Isle of Man the young heroine learns to look outward to find her beauty.

Alexander uses a traditional fantasy device to end his time travel adventure story. He puts a physical break in the text and then begins, "Jason raised his head from his pillow. The black cat, stretched full length beside him, looked up and yawned. Jason rubbed his eyes. His bedroom was just as it had always been. Sunlight poured through the window. How long had he slept?" (*Time Cat*, 190). Typical of the fantasy of Lewis Carroll and C. S. Lewis, this book ends with the boy and cat unable to communicate, yet the boy believes that he really experienced the adventures and finds a T-shaped piece of metal in his pocket as proof. He muses that he has never seen it before, then hears his mother call him to supper and returns to his familiar everyday world. Alexander will not use again the dream-vision in his remaining fantasies. They are depicted as real journeys in a fantastic but realistically developed world.

Still, Alexander had written an "art form" fantasy with many of the elements of style and characterization he used in his later writing. His use of description to introduce a scene, his adroit conversation, and his stock characters are found in subsequent stories. The stories contain a traveling salesman who sells his wares from a wagon, some very talkative young heroines, arrogant rulers, and sinister advisers. His technique of ending episodes with new beginnings is found in his later books.

Once *Time Cat* was completed, Alexander began writing the Prydain series. After its completion, he wrote two more fantasies with magical cats as central characters. Each of these books represents a break in Alexander's style.

The Cat Who Wished to Be a Man

The first, *The Cat Who Wished to Be a Man*, is a full-length children's novel with one group of characters and one central plot. Published in the same year as *The Foundling and Other Tales of Prydain*, it shares commonalities in theme and stylistic mimicking of literary fairy tales by authors such as Hans Christian Andersen. However, *The Cat Who Wished to Be a Man* manipulates folkloric patterns and characters in a style that is appreciated by young readers. This book does not allude to another series of adventures. The action is contained in one simple plot, much like the earlier fairy tales. The story has a happily-ever-after ending. Therefore, the book-length story of a cat who becomes a man does not need a sequel or an introduction to be effective.

Alexander has read existentialist authors and translated Sartre; he was aware of despair in adult writing. He has acknowledged the need in children's literature for an ending that faces reality in a positive way and separates it from adult literature. When discussing the future of adult literature with Dee Stuart, he suggested that it was going too far toward the absurd, leaving little hope for its readers. Children's literature, he added, has a sense of hope that keeps it alive. He went on to say, "A writer in the broadest sense is a teacher to the extent that he presents his own attitude toward people and events; his view of the world. He must have something to say. . . . He must take a moral and ethical stand. If he doesn't his work will be merely works of the intellect without emotional feelings behind them."[3]

His literary fairy tales in *The Foundling and Other Tales of Prydain* contain a good deal of despair. This is the first of his books to dwell on the absurd side of humanity, and, based on Alexander's discussion, it is perhaps his most adultlike children's book. Many of the stories are tragic. They contain twentieth-century political and social messages, but the messages must be interpreted by the reader since they are indirectly presented. Many of the messages would not be deciphered by youthful readers.

Those stories read like warnings or cries for social and political change. Because of their tone and connotations, these short tales stand outside of Alexander's other writings for children. While the stories are successful, they do not contain Alexander's voice as a children's author. They are probably his last "adult writings," though he has categorized them as children's stories.

In *The Cat Who Wished to Be a Man* Alexander changes from the voice of despair to a voice of cautious optimism. His warnings are presented in satirical form, allowing them to both entertain and instruct.

The story is a long parody of the classical beast epics. Lionel, the main character, is a cat involved in a satiric show of human behavior. He has been changed into a man by his master, Magister Stephanus, a magician who earlier gave Lionel speech so that he could have someone to communicate with. Stephanus cannot stand people, and so when Lionel asks to be a man, he suggests that Lionel choose something nicer than man, saying, "You shall be—oh, let us say, a badger. For a few days. A refreshing change. Or an otter? A bird of some sort? Whatever you prefer."[4]

Stephanus wants Lionel to understand that men aren't worth his time, and he wants him to realize that in the end he will return to his life as a cat. But, unlike some transformation stories, in Alexander's fantasy world, Lionel reaches his goal by shapeshifting. When Lionel first becomes a man, he is still a cat in attitudes and behavior. As such, he already is more ethical than the humans he meets. Unlike the beasts who learn from their follies in the beast epics, Alexander's beast teaches the humans he meets about their follies. He remains above reproach in his honesty, loyalty, and courage.

Alexander's interest in cats has led him to believe that some catlike behavior is superior to human decorum. He also projects human responses on his cats and imagines that cats are almost human because of their behavior. In *My Five Tigers* he states, "Cats make an impression on us which we fortify and elaborate with our own imaginations. It is no crime, and we love them all the more because of it" (*Tigers,* 35). The same play with the imagination is seen in *The Cat Who Wished to Be a Man.*

In the book, Alexander allows the cat-turned-man to retain its abilities and tendencies. The reader quickly senses that Lionel's catlike beginnings shape his personality. Since he has known only one man, and that man has always treated him kindly, he trusts those people he meets. The villain Swaggart tells Lionel, "There's rogues in Brightford itching to get their fingers on a man's gold," and then adds, "But don't worry. I'll see you're well looked after" (*Cat Who Wished,* 21). Immediately, Swaggart takes Lionel off to the jail where he "sells" him several town "licenses." Once he has taken all of Lionel's money, he tells him that he can get a good meal from Mistress Gillian. Swaggart assures the innocent Lionel, "All you do is take her by the waist and give her a good, round, lip-smacking kiss" (*Cat Who Wished,* 24). Mistress Gillian, it turns out, is not pleased. Yet, Lionel refuses to be discouraged, even when people prove to be dishonest and immoral.

Alexander is using the cat in his story to show superiority in animal trust and morals. Many of the humans are treacherous and up to no good. Lionel is innocent, trustful, and anxious to please. Even after several misadventures in the village, Lionel refuses to believe that men are inherently bad. When the town mayor, the true villain in the story, is caught in a fire that consumes Gillian's inn, he promises Lionel to reform. Once saved, however, the mayor tries to arrest them:

> "But—but you promised you'd rebuild the inn!" cried Lionel, holding Gillian closer. "And what about the toll gate? What about your gold?"
> Grimy and disheveled, his robe still smoldering where sparks had burned holes in it, Pursewig folded his arms and snorted indignantly:
> "I said nothing of the kind." (*Cat Who Wished*, 96)

Throughout the book, Lionel displays catlike characteristics. He bounds the toll bridge gate—although any ordinary man would break his neck jumping over it—chases away the rats that have been placed in the inn's basement, and springs at his foes when he is cornered. Yet, no one, not even Gillian, will believe he truly is a cat. When she finds out that he is, she admits, "I didn't believe him" (103). Because he is loyal, honest, and gullible, the townspeople think he is a simpleton. Thus, Alexander points out that these qualities are not considered admirable by humanity.

The honest people in the story fit into Alexander's evolving cast of characters. The young woman Gillian is a typical female heroine. She is at odds with society and is outspoken. She is willing to sacrifice for others. Dr. Tudbelly is a charlatan who uses Latin-sounding speech and trickery to get what he wants. Tudbelly helps Lionel and Gillian, though his interest in helping begins for selfish reasons. He is Lionel's chief aide.

A feeling of absurdity does exist in this story. The wizard Stephanus is distrustful of humans and is self-centered enough to want his way without regard for others. Lionel trusts all people, even when they deceive him time and again.

In the end, Stephanus argues, "My cat is not a person. . . . Furthermore, since he belongs to me—" (*Cat Who Wished*, 104), but when he cannot change Lionel into a cat, he tells him that he must leave unless he is willing to lose his memory of the world of people. Lionel chooses human society, as Alexander does. The book takes Alexander's three protagonists—Lionel, Gillian, and Dr. Tudbelly—away from the world of spells and back to humanity.

There will be one other wizard in Alexander's book-length fantasies, and he will be more out of step than Stephanus. Both can be seen as an existentialist who look at the world of man in despair and who wish to leave it behind them. Both are disgusted with society and see no hope for it unless man changes. While they may hold some of Alexander's own cynicism, they do not represent him.

It is clear that Alexander's alter ego is the flimflam man. As a child, Alexander flimflammed his teachers into believing he was ill; as an adult he flimflams readers into believing that what they read is real. Some of his characters are filmflam men. Dr. Tudbelly is typical. He tricks the villagers into believing that Gillian is making a dish called "Pro Bono Publico" for them, then cajoles them into giving ingredients for the meal. The flimflam man, a purely American invention, becomes a focal figure in *The Cat Who Wished to Be a Man*. He differs from Fflewddur Fflam who is not as cynical, but both are storytellers. Dr. Tudbelly, however, is a trickster who sees the world for what it is and makes it as good a place as he can, relying on man's need for optimism and dreams. The character type will return as Count Las Bombas in the Westmark series to add much needed comic relief from a story filled with despair.

Although *The Cat Who Wished to Be a Man* is cynical about humanity, its message of despair is couched in humor. As is common with Alexander, this book ends with an uncertain but hopeful new beginning for human society.

The Town Cats

Alexander's second book with personified cats, *The Town Cats and Other Tales*, is a series of short stories. It resembles *Time Cat* because it is episodic and contains a vast array of characters and settings that differ from story to story. This time, however, there are no central characters who appear in all of the adventures. Each story is complete in itself.[5]

The stories work much the way the medieval beast epic tales do. The main heroes are cats, and their adventures constitute a sustained satire on certain human foibles. In all but one of the stories, the cats and the humans can communicate with each other, and they treat each other as equals. In the end, however, the cats are superior beings who solve the humans' problems. As such, they resemble the cat in Perrault's famous fairy tale "Puss in Boots." Because the tales focus on moral dilemmas, they read like animal fables. Their protagonists are clever cats. The humans suffer from vanity, false values, and pretentiousness. The cats must teach them to behave in new ways. Throughout, Alexander repeats the moral, be yourself; don't give in to arrogance. Always, he uses satire. For instance, in "The Cat Who Said No" the ruler Shira-Zar has never been told that he has a bad idea. Alexander writes, "Indeed, no matter how extravagant his commands even in matters of state, his Grand Vizier and Royal Council always hailed them as utterances of unmatched wisdom."[6] In addition, his subjects will not let him lose in chess. At last, he tires of his royal partners and has Baraka, the cat of the Shaipur Bazaar, summoned to play against him. Baraka is not pleased by the royal invitation. He feels it is his business to keep his eyes on the activities of the bazaar and to converse with the people of the bazaar and the visiting scholars. Alexander continues, "Baraka could not turn down a game of chess, whomever the opponent, and, knowing the skill of Shira-Zar, he expected this to be a short one" (*Town Cats*, 38). When the cat finds the ruler cheating, he calmly points out that something is amiss. No amount of cajoling will change the cat's mind. Baraka delivers Alexander's moral, telling Shira-Zar, "It would seem to me, O Uncontradictable One, that an honest 'No' is worth more than a false 'Yes'" (*Town Cats*, 47).

In the last story of the collection, "The Apprentice Cat," Alexander has a woman and her husband try to make their cat into something he isn't. This is the only tale in the book that contains a cat who cannot talk to humans. In the end, Alexander reminds his audience that cats are really only cats, adding, "In itself . . . a quite remarkable achievement" (*Town Cats*, 126).

This story signals another shift in Alexander's writing. *The Town Cats and Other Tales* is a transitional book that allowed Alexander to poke fun at humanity and to pay tribute to the qualities he admires in cats. Much like the old couple in "The Apprentice Cat," Alexander placed human values on cats because that is what he wished to see. After the book's completion, he determined to go past his reveries and to seek a new form of fiction that could contain his existential ideas. While Alexander could have written more tales in this style, he chose not to, because he felt a need to branch out again, trying another generic pattern and incorporating the best elements from these tales in his writing.

5

Writing Parables

Lloyd Alexander did not intentionally write picture book fantasies after finishing the Prydain series. He had no interest in writing books for the young child. His intended child audience had
been the adolescent, and his first short stories, including *The
Foundling and Other Tales of Prydain, Coll and His White Pig,*
and *The Truthful Harp,* were written with that audience in mind.
Those lengthy short stories were meant to complete the Prydain
series for the reader who already knew the characters from the
longer books. Yet, shortly after the Prydain series was completed,
Alexander plunged into writing a different kind of short tale—
picture book stories that stood on their own.

During the seventies Alexander wrote these three picture-book
stories designed to appeal to a different audience. They have
some commalities. They each could have been set elsewhere; the
settings have been determined by the artists' interpretations, not
by the author; none of the stories addresses a typical problem
facing the young child; their implied audience is a more sophisticated one; unlike Alexander's other stories, these tales are
openly moralistic and allegorical; all three have been illustrated
by artists Alexander respected. Although two of the books were
suggested to Alexander, the stories are distinctly his.

Published in 1971 and 1972, respectively, *The King's Fountain* and *The Four Donkeys* evolved from discussions with friends. The last story, *The Fortunetellers,* was written about the same time, but it sat in his attic for more than ten years before Alexander unearthed it and sent it off to his editor. The three book formats are unique in settings and art styles. Yet, though the books were not designed to be used together, they work visually as a set, and the stories seem to be parts of a unified whole.

The King's Fountain

When Lloyd Alexander was visiting children's artist/author Ezra Jack Keats, Keats showed him some acrylic paintings that he hoped to incorporate into a story. He asked Alexander how the pictures might work into a folkloric tale, and Alexander suggested the basic plot for *The King's Fountain*. Alexander was impressed by the textual richness of the paintings and was pleased when Keats asked him if he would write the story. It gave him a chance to work with an artist he respected and to try out a new writing style.

Both agreed that the inspiration of the story came from the Hebrew texts. They turned to Hillel's "If I am not for myself, who will be for me? And if I am only for myself, what am I? And if not now, when?" The illustrations and references to Hillel determined Alexander's setting and tone. The story had to contain a Jewish flavor, and the tale had to reveal Hebrew teachings. Alexander wanted to explore the topic of personal discovery in "the form and flavor of the Hebrew parables or ancient Sufi teaching stories."[1]

Set in ancient times, the plot revolves around a king's selfishness. He wishes to build a fountain and give himself eternal fame. However, the fountain will stop the flow of the water to the common people living in the city below his palace. One of the poor men realizes that the fountain will cause deprivation and death and he tries to find someone who can warn the king. In traditional fairy-tale form, the poor man turns to others who are more respected in the kingdom. They offer no useful advice, however.

Once they fail to meet his needs, he returns home. Alexander
writes:

> His daughter spoke then, and said:
>   "But, Father—why not go yourself?"
> Confused, unable to answer, the poor man looked at
> the faces of his wife and family. At last, he bowed his
> head and murmured:
>   "I hear my own flesh and blood. Indeed, there is no one
> else, and I myself must go to the King." (*Fountain,* n.p.)

The humble man is given an audience with the king and is able
to persuade him that the fountain is wrong. The fountain is never
built, and the story of the poor man and the king becomes an oral
hero legend for the country's people. Alexander ends his story by
stating that the scholar's long account of the events has been lost,
and oral tales have highly embellished the poor man's deed. Thus,
though there is no proof of the event, the king and poor man remain in legend.

Written in true allegorical form, the characters represent attitudes not expressly stated in the text. This conventional stereo-
typing helps shape the tale's messages: the poor man can see
what the rich cannot see; the king is not concerned with the fate
of those under his rule unless it affects him; the wise men cannot
express their ideas to the common people; the merchants care for
nothing but wealth; the strong man would use brute force rather
than discuss matters; the daughter has the wisdom of the innocent child and can see obvious answers to adult problems. In the
end, the king tells the poor man that he is more wise, eloquent,
and brave than the others.

Alexander's writing is carefully controlled, tightly constructed,
folkloric in form. The story contains a repetitive pattern of events
that reinforce the idea that, like David and Goliath, the weak can
stand against the mighty. The hero is a common man, easily accepted by the listener. He is never described as more than "a poor
man," yet the listener knows instinctively what he is like. In folkloric tradition, the poor man tells the listener how to respond to

each character by musing about each of his encounters. The musings are stylistic, and they sound like repetitive rhymes. For instance, when the poor man leaves the company of the scholar, he says, "Alas, the grandest thought quenches no thirst. Besides, what good is all the learning in the world if there is no one who can understand it?" Each time he begins by saying "alas" and follows with a simile. The merchants' fine words are "empty air without a brave heart," and the strong man's hand is "useless without a wise head to guide it." This is followed with an epigram. Of the merchants he asks, "What good is a golden tongue without a brave heart?" and of the brave man he muses, "What good is all the bravery in the world if it serves no purpose?" Poetic in style, the book fleshes out simple cultural beliefs without seeming to be didactic.

The Four Donkeys

The Four Donkeys was not originally planned as a picture book story. Rather, George Nicholson, then an editor at Holt, Rinehart, and Winston, suggested that Alexander write a textbook story, using the same events told from different points of view. He hoped to show children how point of view works in fiction.

The idea appealed to Alexander; he decided to try to write a modern-day version of the fable "The Miller, His Son and the Donkey." His version, however, would be peopled with characters who were not related. They would display differences in occupations, attitudes, and goals. Each would have a distinct personality, and each would begin by looking at life from his perspective. Thus, *The Four Donkeys* is a study of character development.

Alexander begins his story by introducing his three antiheroes: the tailor, the shoemaker, and the baker. They are depicted as self-centered men who wish to show the world their importance. The tailor has no respect for either the shoemaker or the baker. He feels the baker is silly in his flamboyant clothes. Alexander shows the tailor's contempt by having him mutter, "True, I made the thing [his jacket] for him in the first place. But only because he'd have it no other way."[2] Once on the road, the tailor's shoes pinch him and he is forced to sit down. He complains, "I can thank the Shoemaker for my pains. . . . Oh, he's a fine cobbler, if you like bunions and blisters!" The shoemaker considers the tailor and the baker a pair of fools. He believes the shoes he made the tailor are masterpieces, and he begrudges paying the baker for a ride to the fair. The baker admires himself in his jacket, and he plans to design a hat and a pair of shoes (which will be made by the shoemaker) to go with it. It is obvious that he feels he is the only real craftsman.

The fourth personality in the story, the four-legged donkey, is mistreated by the humans who never look at events from any perspective other than their own. As the story develops, the donkey balks at their insensitivity. His behavior forces the three men to help each other. They agree to cart the donkey and their wares to the fair in the baker's wagon. Acting as beasts of burden, they pull the load. Alexander writes:

> For some while, deep in their own miseries, they only glared at each other. Then the Tailor stumbled and would have fallen flat on his face. The Baker grudgingly reached out a burly arm to help him along. The Tailor was too surprised to do more than gasp "Thank you," and he was all the more astonished when the Baker actually grinned at him.
>
> Limping on, however, the Tailor's feet began smarting worse than ever. "Now," he moaned, "there's not enough room in my shoes for my blisters!"
>
> They halted a moment and, without even being asked, the Shoemaker, a little less gruff than he had been, softened the Tailor's shoes with some oil.

By the end, they learn how the others feel, begin to help one another, and gain more from their trip than they would have had they arrived at the fair in time to sell their wares.

The Four Donkeys resembles European folktales where foolish men learn how to behave through circumstances beyond their control. The plot contains the typical circular pattern, and the tone remains lighthearted. Alexander's implied reader perceives the humor in the events and understands the irony in the men's first evaluations of one another. The text contains several predictable twists of fate. The older reader is aware that these men experience personal change by the end of their trip and understands that the plot is less important than the character development.

When the story was finished, Alexander and Nicholson agreed that it was too sophisticated to be the textbook exercise Nicholson had suggested. And so, the story ended up in a picture book. Its audience is varied. Readers familiar with the European folktale about the miller and his donkey will enjoy the subtle rewriting. Adults will enjoy the obvious irony in the various points of view. Young children will enjoy it simply as a good story. *School Library Journal's* review stated, "This is the perfect read-aloud for second or third graders and is sophisticated enough to attract fourth- and fifth-grade readers."[3] Like Alexander's previous stories, the book best fits an older audience who would understand the unstated ironies.

The Fortunetellers

Since his early days, Alexander has drawn satirical cartoons. He also was intrigued with the one- or two-paragraph fable, which could be paradoxical and ironic. He wrote *The Fortunetellers* to see if he could create a fable to illustrate. Somehow, the story and his notes about its creation ended up in his attic. When he recovered it, he sent it to Ann Durrell, and she suggested that it would make an excellent picture book. This time, Alexander asked if artist Trina Schart Hyman, a longtime friend, could do the illustrations. She is currently working on the project, and has placed the story in Africa. Alexander is excited about the prospect since he feels that Hyman "remembers the personalities in the stories."

The Fortunetellers is a humorous short story that deals with man's simplistic desire to understand his fate. In this story, Alexander's soothsayer is not able to foretell the future but can suggest what his listener might do to fulfill his dreams. Again, Alexander uses humor to cover up his didactic message. He, ironically, suggests that those who are unable to live in uncertainty will accept any prediction of the future as long as they are told what they wish to hear.

Alexander develops *The Fortunetellers* in a conversational style that reminds the listener of the Jewish tales about Gimpel the fool or the Turkish stories about the Hodja. The story's protagonist is a simpleton, a young carpenter who travels to a neighboring town in order to hear from a traveling fortuneteller what his future will hold. Alexander writes:

> "My first prediction is this," the fortuneteller said, before the carpenter could begin. "You're going to pay me a nice fee. But that's a mere trifle to someone destined for wealth."
>
> "Do you see me rich, then?" exclaimed the carpenter, gladly handing over the coins the fortuneteller demanded.
>
> "Rich you will surely be," answered the fortuneteller, settling his tall cap on his head and gazing into the crystal ball on the table. "On one condition: that you earn large sums of money."
>
> "Marvelous!" cried the carpenter. "Things look brighter already. And with so much wealth—will I be famous, too?"
>
> "No question about it," said the fortuneteller, "once you become well known."
>
> "Amazing!" said the carpenter. "But, now, tell me: Will I marry and be happy ever after?"
>
> "You shall wed your true love," said the fortuneteller, "if you find her and she agrees; and be happy as any in the world if you can avoid being miserable."[4]

When the carpenter returns to see the fortuneteller a second time, the man is gone. The villagers, however, mistake the carpenter for the soothsayer, and, remembering the words said to him, he takes up the occupation. Thus, all of the earlier predictions come true.

As a twist of fate, Alexander has the first fortuneteller meet chance circumstances that cause his demise. Alexander ends by telling his audience that the carpenter was always grateful to the fortuneteller for what he learned. The mature audience understands the ironic joke. Even those who pretend to see the future cannot predict what it holds. And, those who trust their fortunes learn to depend upon "signs" for their success.

All three tales deal with common human attitudes and with man's need to accept the fact that events cannot be controlled but they can be modified. In *The King's Fountain* Alexander suggests that even the smallest man can intervene and cause change if he looks beyond himself for answers to impending disasters. Readers of *The Four Donkeys* will see that people who are self-centered and egotistical can become more humane if they look beyond their own needs. And, finally, *The Fortunetellers* implies that life is what we make of it.

The lessons presented are ones best understood by Alexander's adolescent audience. These three books neatly tie together some of Alexander's most important messages. Because of their brevity and tone, the stories are more obviously didactic than any of his other writings. Their short form and adult tone place them in the literary fairy-tale genre. They resemble the works of Hans Christian Andersen. Each is complete in itself, yet together they express the attitudes and concerns of their creator.

6

Emerging Patterns

Alexander once commented that readers often write and ask for sequels to *The Wizard in the Tree, The Marvelous Misadventures of Sebastian,* and *The First Two Lives of Lukas-Kasha.* He remarked, "The adventures don't need follow-ups, you know. The readers can supply them themselves." Indirectly, however, Alexander has fulfilled those requests. All three of the books are direct links to Alexander's later multiple volumed series concerning Westmark and Vesper. They contain emerging patterns that will be perfected in the two later series. Although the Westmark and Vesper heroes and heroines have different names and more carefully honed individual personalities, they closely resemble the characters found in the earlier adventures.

The Marvelous Misadventures of Sebastian

After the 1970 publication of Alexander's *The Marvelous Misadventures of Sebastian,* the book was heralded as a fantasy. In *Horn Book* Paul Heins called it "a comic fantasy" that could be "read as an allegory on the ambivalent power of beauty."[1] The book is still usually labeled a fantasy. Zena Sutherland placed it in the fantastic genre in her 1986 edition of *Children and Books,* though she acknowledged that the fantasy was "slight" and depended upon "the exaggeration of reality rather than the creation of a new world or supernatural beings."[2]

At the time of publication, Alexander suggested that he did not think it was another fantasy. When he was discussing the book with the editors of *School Library Journal,* he called it "a comedy in the broad sense." The book, he said, was "about creativity, about Art, about discovering what is really involved in creation."[3]

The Marvelous Misadventures of Sebastian is primarily a comedy; more specifically, it is a comedy of manners. Set in the early eighteenth century, the story abounds with courtiers, traveling entertainers, and political intrigue. The plot cleverly interweaves a series of escapades involving a young violinist who loses his courtly position, a superior cat who seems more capable of solving problems than the young hero, a princess fleeing a prearranged wedding, a motley crew of actors, and a notorious rebel captain who turns out to be less than what rumors suggest. All are loosely joined together by a mutual desire get rid of the country's Regent, a wicked man who will rule with or without the princess at his side.

While the characters' witty conversations and inane posturing add humor to the story, they are not memorable personalities. The story's construction holds the reader's interest. The overall comical mood and a continuous string of highly improbable events amuse the reader. The entire tone is highly satirical, and the action is almost burlesque. Yet, Alexander has something to say. He is interested in exploring what it takes to be a real artist and why humans act in unpredictable, illogical, and foppish ways.

The story begins at Baron Purn-Hessel's pretentious, courtly estate. Sebastian, a court fiddler, lives in a wing of the mansion that houses the Baron's musicians. Alexander shows the reader that the Baron can hardly afford his musicians, especially since he is subject to constant taxes levied by the monarchy. The Royal Treasurer and First Minister of Finance, a man who is "monstrously fat, with great slabs of jowls and a mouth as wide as a toad's"[4] arrives to collect a fee for the Regent, who plans to marry Princess Isabel. He remarks, "The Regent allows you the privilege

of offering, shall we say, a personal gift—in addition to the cus-
tomary tokens of esteem" (*Sebastian,* 3). The Baron knows he
cannot afford the gift, but he agrees to pay and calls his musicians
together to entertain his guest. Thus, Alexander has set up a
kingdom of monetary extravagance.

Sebastian plays a sound "like the rasp of cloth tearing down the
middle" (*Sebastian,* 5), embarrasses the Royal Treasurer, is forced
into exile, and so, becomes a traveling minstrel. Alexander has
exposed the false airs of the court and has placed his hero outside
of the system.

Outside the court, Sebastian discovers that things are seldom
what they seem. He stops at a small town and enters an inn, "The
Merry Host of Dorn," with its "painting of a hearty, apple-cheeked
face grinning broadly, with one eye shut in a jolly wink" (*Sebastian,* 11). The real innkeeper is "a gaunt, stoop-shouldered man
in a soiled apron, a dour, scowling fellow with a sharp jaw and
close-set eyes" (*Sebastian,* 12). Sebastian bargains for a position
as the inn's fiddler, but before he can begin he gets involved in a
local brawl over a cat who has been caught in a snare. Two local
villagers are planning its demise. Alexander's brings the scene
alive, saying:

> Foul with mire, blood-spattered, one ear torn, the cat
> hissed, spat furiously, and flung itself against the net,
> screaming and thrusting its claws through the mesh as
> if it meant to repay its abusers even at the cost of its own
> life.
>
> "What's this?" cried Sebastian. "What are you doing to
> that poor cat?"
>
> ..."Cat?" cried Skimmerhorn. "You're a bigger fool
> than you look. That's no cat! The vile brute's a witch!"
> (*Sebastian,* 15–16)

The townsmen declare that the cat is able to take any shape it
wishes. One man says that the cat is black, a true sign of evilness.
Sebastian replies, "If you don't count the dirt, he looks altogether
white to me," and is told:

"Yes, and there's the slyness of him," said Spargel. "To
show himself white and put honest folk off their guard.
But you can be sure, secretly he's black as pitch."

"That's common sense," a townsman agreed, solemnly
nodding his head. "If it was me who was a black witch-
cat, I'd let none find out. But for all his cunning, he's
given himself away. I've seen gray-striped, mustard, and
piebald cats, but never a white, blue-eyed one like this.
Unnatural, that's what he is, as any fool can see." (*Sebastian,* 17–18)

Sebastian saves the cat, but his nose and violin are broken, along
with the Merry Host's window. Once more, Sebastian is on the
road, but now the cat travels on his shoulders.

Although it is easy to see that the cat is in charge of Sebastian,
the fiddler calls the cat "his" and tells him, "You deserve a gold
saucer! A silken pillow! And more! Well, you'll have them, somehow, and there's my word on it!" (*Sebastian,* 97). The contrast between Sebastian's impoverished condition and his comments adds
to the story's irony.

Like many of the classical comedies of manners, *The Marvelous
Misadventures of Sebastian* involves disguises and deceit. The notorious captain is "a stout little man" with "ruddy cheeks . . . as
plump as those of the cherubs painted on Baron Purn-Hessel's
ceiling, his sparse brown hair hung down about his ears, and he
blinked around him with a pair of blue eyes as innocent and guile-
less as a baby's" (*Sebastian,* 32). Yet, a farmer describes him as
"the very devil of a fellow, tall as a tree, with a great black mus-
tache," only to be contradicted by another who says he is "yellow-
haired" with eyes that "flash like blue lightning" (*Sebastian,* 42).
The captain later explains,

Ah—as for that, none of my doing, you can be sure.
Tongues wag, one thing piles on top of another. And all
the more, as most of the Captain's staunchest followers
have never seen him. But if it suits them to match him
to their fancy, if it pleases them to believe he's dark or

> he's fair, tall or short, I daresay there's no harm one way
> or the other. . . . I should even say, in a manner of speak-
> ing, that anyone who does his part for a measure of jus-
> tice in the Principality—why, he himself is the Captain,
> without even knowing it. (*Sebastian,* 166–67)

The captain is a master of deception, and he is able to see what others do not. He notices that the young boy with whom Sebastian tries to sleep in the Golden Stag is actually the princess-in-exile. Once she opens her mouth it is obvious she is not what she seems. Princess Isabel uses plural pronouns when discussing herself. Her speech is flowery and unnatural. When first discovered, she says, "Sir, in future and presumably more favorable circumstances, your courtesy shall be both gratefully remembered and appropriately recompensed. Be assured also that the emptying of that receptacle was the result of momentary confusion, and should not be construed as indicating ill intent or deliberate malice. However, since you offer to be of service, your most accommodating and expedient course will be, sir, to depart from these premises" (*Sebastian,* 54).

While Captain Freeling recognizes the princess for her royal rank through her speech and demeanor, others either take her at face value or "discover" that she is a girl for the obvious physical reasons. Only one other person, Alexander's villainous assassin, seems capable of recognizing her.

Alexander's story is a comedy of mistaken identities. It is a satire with enough clues for the reader to unravel the events and disguises. Alexander's plot and descriptions allow the reader to discover the characters' true identities before Sebastian.

Alexander combines the adventures of his youthful hero and heroine with those of a traveling company called the Gallimaufry-Theatricus. Master Quicksilver and his wife Madame Sophie are in charge of the company. Quicksilver is a master at applying greasepaint and creating new appearances. Sebastian good-naturedly accuses Quicksilver of being a brazen hoaxer, and Quicksilver replies that the world is better off for its ability to disregard reality when it listens to a story. Once again, Alexander confirms his allegiance to the flimflam man. Quicksilver, however, seems as caught up in fantasy as the next person. When Madame Sophie first discovers that Sebastian's boy servant is a girl, Quicksilver paints the typical plot, saying, "Your families were against the match. And the two of you, head over heels in love! What else to do but to run off to be wed!" (*Sebastian*, 116–7). Sebastian muses, "Where does the world begin and the Gallimaufry-Theatricus leave off? The Princess—from lackey to dancing girl to blushing bride-to-be! And Quicksilver . . . takes us for a pair of lovers, and I think he'll see us that way no matter what I tell him! Whatever gave him the notion, I can't imagine. Unless he's been in the Theatricus so long that he can't tell truth from moonshine. Or, indeed, is all of it moonshine?" (*Sebastian*, 118).

In the end the flimflam man is right. The princess and the fiddler fall in love and plan to get married. Through his comedy of manners Alexander illustrates how misinterpretation and deceit, combined with cultural etiquette, can cause chaos, resulting in a new pattern of behavior.

The book is also an exploration of the creation of art. Sebastian begins by playing the violin, but once it is broken on the road, he joins the traveling company and is given a new, "magical" violin that will play only for a "master musician worthy of the instrument" (*Sebastian*, 95). Sebastian hears the music he plays, begins to feel it in new ways, and creates new music. He seems to be controlled by the fiddle; when he is playing he is oblivious to the rest of the world. He has no interest in eating, sees no one about him, and loses all sense of time. He is dangerously, self-destructedly absorbed in creating new sounds. Sebastian believes that the fiddle creates the music throughout most of the book, but when he is forced to play for the Regent he gains the hero's understanding. The music is a part of him. Sebastian says, "One thing the fiddle taught me: before, music was my living; now it's my life" (*Sebastian*, 201).

The book ends with a new beginning for its hero and heroine. The fiddler is leaving the court to seek experience and a voice of his own, and the princess is staying behind until she can hand the kingdom over to her people. It also ends with a change in

Alexander's writing. Earlier he had relied upon the remnants of past legends. Now, he creates characters in a plot structure that relies upon archetypal patterns but which renews those patterns. His use of the formulas earlier employed by Shakespeare and the early authors of the comedy of manners has gone undetected by experts in children's literature. Thus, while the structure of his novel resembles these earlier classics, Alexander has skillfully adapted them into a style of his own.

The characters are prototypes for the people who are engaged in a similar courtly struggle in the Westmark series. However, the Westmark characters will have more three-dimensional personalities, and they will appear in a serious drama, not in high comedy.

The Wizard in the Tree

The Wizard in the Tree was written after *The Marvelous Misadventures of Sebastian* but is closely linked to the earlier Prydain books. Set in a distant time, the book draws upon Celtic fantasy motifs. Alexander has placed a wizard, a talking pig, and a young female protagonist who saves the countryside from ruin in the story. At the same time, new images and devices are being introduced, and Alexander is displaying a new projection of fantasy. This time, the wizard Arbican is not a mythic hero. He is crotchety and sarcastic and not impressed with human fairy tales and legends. He suggests that beliefs in magic and wishful thinking are devices used by humans to help them get through their ordinary lives. In addition, there is no bildungsroman hero in these adventures. The story does not create a better world, and the ending is less satisfying than some of Alexander's earlier books. Like the Westmark series, *The Wizard in the Tree* ends with an uncertain future for the heroine. There is a sense of longing for things to be different. Finally, *The Wizard in the Tree*'s setting and events link the story to historical and social commentary, not to mythology and romance.

Booklist's review noted, "the handful of Dickensian characters—a murderous squire, cookshop shrew, kind-but-weak husband, fair-minded notary, and miscellany of country folk—plays out a script graced with quotable bits of wisdom about the real nature of magic."[5] This is a bridging book from fantasy to historical realism that allows Alexander to explore the writing techniques attributed to Charles Dickens, a favorite from his childhood.

The heroine of the book is a young orphan, Mallory, who is working as a scullery maid for the Parsels. Like many of Charles Dickens's child caretakers, Mrs. Parsel keeps the child to do her dirty work, all the time complaining of the burden she has to endure. Not quite a villain, Mrs. Parsel is very much a ruthless scoundrel who misuses the child in her custody. Mr. Parsel is thin and henpecked. He likes Mallory, but he does not stand up for her until the end of the book. The notary public is a man of the law. He may not like what is happening to his village, and indirectly to Mallory, but he will not interfere unless the law is broken. Thus, Alexander depicts Victorian characters like the ones Dickens developed in *David Copperfield, Oliver Twist, The Old Curiosity Shop,* and *Great Expectations.* There are few real heroes in this story, and, while the unsavory ordinary people may not be totally corrupt, they bend the law whenever they can. The squire's gamekeeper poaches on the estate, and the heroine recognizes that he is unscrupulous.

Alexander also mimics Dickens's technique of providing comic relief by introducing scenes filled with homespun simpletons. Although these humorous scenes cause a break in the main action, they do not detract from the plot but alter the story's pace or direction. When, for instance, Arbican has escaped with Mallory from the squire's house, a wild chase scene ensues, and the story switches from the squire's wickedness to Arbican's plight. Alexander must get his two protagonists back into the main action, and he does it in a diverting episode that seems unconnected to the rest of the plot.

Arbican, after changing into a pig, is discovered talking to Mallory. The scene itself is one of comic relief, but it allows Alexander to develop Mallory's personality. She is frustrated with the yokels'

discussion about the pig's ability to talk and angry at their attempts to have the pig as their own. She faces the two farmers
without considering whether she will be hurt as she tries to protect Arbican. When the young fool overhears her talking with Arbican, she insists he is wrong, pigs can't talk. Alexander employs
doubletalk, having the boy remember that his "old dad" once saw
a bird who could talk. Alexander continues:

> "That's a poll-parrot," said Mallory. "They're supposed to
> talk; everyone knows that."
> "Right!" exclaimed Burdick, his face lighting up. "So
> this will be a poll-piggy!"
> "No!" cried Mallory. "It's no kind of pig at all."
> "If it isn't," replied Burdick, "then it's the ugliest,
> nakedest baby I've ever seen." . . . determined to study
> this remarkable animal at closer range, [he] seized the
> plump cheeks in both hands.
> "Stop that immediately," snapped Arbican, pulling his
> head free of Burdick's grip. "I may have no say about my
> shape, but I'm not required to be pinched and prodded
> by some ignorant rustic who calls me ugly into the
> bargain!"
> Mallory threw her hands up in despair. (*Wizard*, 81–
> 82)

This humorous digression is linked into the main plot by Burdick's old dad who regularly supplies Parsel with his vegetables
in the past. The father is familiar with Mallory and tells her that
the pig can't be hers because "Parsel don't keep pigs" (*Wizard*, 87).
The discussion allows Alexander to play with words while showing Mallory's exasperation. Once Burdick and his father determine that the pig is not a poll-piggy, they decide to kill it. When
Mallory stands in the way, Burdick attacks Mallory. Alexander
has her stand her ground, writing, "Trembling though she was,
she looked Burdick boldly in the eyes, hoping her fear showed less
than her determination" (*Wizard*, 93).

The scene leads back into the main action by having Mr. Parsel pull up in front of the house and try to help Mallory. Through his timid attempt to save her from danger, Alexander makes him into a sympathetic character and brings the action back to the story's main conflict. Thus Alexander ties several events and characters together within a series of short, seemingly haphazard episodes, a technique he will use in both the Westmark and the Vesper series.

Perhaps the most significant link between this and the books to follow, however, is Alexander's use of stock characters within a social drama, a technique he has credited to Dickens. In 1968 Alexander wrote, "The essence of Dickens was not limited to time, place, or social level [because Dickens was] writing most fundamentally of man's inhumanity to man [as well as] man's humanity to man."[7]

The Wizard in the Tree contains a self-centered villain, Scrupnor, who is willing to help the Parsels upgrade their inn if they will trade only with him. Alexander tells the reader that Scrupnor plans to run any merchants out of town who refuse to sign similar deals. By the end of the book, Squire Scrupnor has killed two men and attempted to kill several others. He is not interested in the welfare of the town's people; he is a heartless villain. Much like the heartless characters in Dickens's Victorian stories, Scrupnor is to be feared and hated, and he brings social issues into the story. He has inherited land through foul play. He intends to industrialize the area by building roads, tearing down the tenant farmers' homes, creating a coal mine, and forcing the village people to work in his sweatshops. He represents all that is bad in big business. The reader cheers when he causes his own death.

Alexander does not dwell on the evils of industrialization, but shows how commerce causes problems for everyone except Mallory and Arbican. Mallory is a typical Dickensian child; she is caught in a dire situation, and she wishes for a happy home. She is able to act heroically, but she is not capable of shaping events. Once everything is put to rights, she inherits the squire's land and becomes the village's heroine. She is the youngest member of the cast, yet she is the most ecologically minded. When she is in charge, she declares, "I certainly won't pull down the cottages for the sake of a coal mine. And Scrupnor's road—the damage is done, but I'll try to mend it somehow" (*Wizard,* 155).

Mallory is also a believer of fantasy. She has always taken more stock in the tales her mother told her than in Scrupnor's materialism. She is not absorbed with Scrupnor's dealings; she is more concerned about helping a wizard than saving the village from Scrupnor's corrupt plans. She acts because Arbican will die if he stays in the world of humans, and she wishes to escape from her everyday world. Mallory needs to believe in something, to feel loved. Yet, she is willing to forsake her personal goals so that she can help others. In the end Mallory's fantasy dreams are not realized. She wishes to travel with Arbican, but she cannot. She longs for fairy-tale happy endings, but she gets none. She has grown up, acquired responsibilities, and must accept reality.

The magic has broken down. Arbican is not a successful wizard. He has been forced to stay behind in man's world for too long, and he has lost almost all of his powers. He is cynical and anxious to leave the world of people behind, allowing them to create whatever fantasies for themselves they need. He continually points out that Mallory is able to save the two of them with her quick wit and her common sense. He listens to the remnants of her mother's fairy tales with disdain. Yet, he encourages Mallory to keep her tales, saying, "Those tales of yours—yes, you people made them up. They aren't tales about *us,* though you may pretend they are. They're tales about yourselves, or at least the best parts of yourselves. They're not true in the outside world, mine or any other. But in the inside, yes, indeed" (*Wizard,* 156).

Through Arbican Alexander reminds his readers that stories are important, that new generations can respond cautiously to the everyday world and look to stories of past heroes to find humane ways to solve their problems. As Alexander's alter ego, Arbican leaves the world of mankind behind. Alexander breaks with the image of the wizard who can live in two worlds at once when Arbican bids his heroine a fond farewell, reminding her, "You have your voyage to make, as I have mine" (*Wizard,* 156).

Alexander considered how stereotypic characters worked for Dickens, and wrote, "Dickens thoroughly understood the literary paradox: that the more specific and individual a character is, the more typical he becomes." It is easy to see Mallory and Arbican in this light. Mallory wants to help others, whatever the cost. Arbican is crotchety and practical and is continually absorbed with his own plight. Yet, both characters are distinctive and very personable.

Alexander has carefully embedded descriptive details in the fast-paced plot of *The Wizard in the Tree* to help the reader identify the villains and the heroes. The same techniques are used again in Alexander's Vesper stories, but they are found in new adventures, which convey distinctive messages about humanity.

The First Two Lives of Lukas-Kasha

In "Fantasy As Images: A Literary View," written after he had finished *The First Two Lives of Lukas-Kasha,* Alexander discusses the common literary elements of imagery, plot, and characterization, and he links fantasy to the more traditional images found in oral tales and in mythology. He continues, "There's another aspect of fantasy—and art in general—I should mention. Perhaps it's the most important: the aspect of playfulness. . . . I use this word in its best and most creative sense, and imply no lack of serious purpose. On the contrary, we, like children, can be seriously playful. There can be tragic as well as comic games. The idea I'm trying to express is that art *plays*. It plays with color, sounds, shapes; with characters and settings; with stories; with ideas and feelings. It plays—but never trifles."[8] Alexander's interpretation of playfulness in writing is important. It is one of the strongest assets of *The First Two Lives of Lukas-Kasha.* Another is his ability to include an important message in a seemingly simple adventure story. Early reviewers noted the book's "colorful encounters" and "playful scenes." Betsy Byars called the book "a work of art," excellent in plot and characterization. In addition, she noted, "any book which makes non-violence attractive and enforces the value of human life has to be taken seriously."[9]

Although fantasy, *The First Two Lives of Lukas-Kasha* varies from Alexander's earlier stories. The setting diverges from his traditionally European backdrop. Instead, the major part of the action takes place within a Persian-like locale. Twice in the past Alexander had used the Middle East as a central setting; in both cases it was in short parables where the plot dominated and the action did not depend upon the foreign setting. In contrast, the setting is an essential element in *The First Two Lives of Lukas-Kasha.*

The lack of traditional fantasy motifs in a major portion of the story also separates this book from his earlier books. Once Lukas-Kasha lands on the beach of Abadan, Alexander dispenses with fantastic events and characters. With the exception of Lukas's trip into an unknown land, all of the events are possible. The characters are not dependent upon the weather, magical objects, or talking beasts. They solve their problems without resorting to fantastic devices. In fact, magic doesn't help. For instance, the astrologer finds that magical incantations and formulas cannot help him predict the future.

The tone is also distinctive. The story seems to be exceptionally lighthearted and whimsical. Yet, there is an air of fatalism throughout. The characterization is more plausible than in Alexander's earlier books. Events seem to happen in coincidental but realistic ways.

The story evolved during Jimmy Carter's presidency. Alexander admired Carter for his humanitarian principles. Egypt (a traditional Arabic country) and Israel (a country with strong Western ties) were beginning to negotiate their now famous peace pact with Carter's assistance. These two states, because of their size and prominence in the news, had come to represent the Middle East cultural conflict, and they were showing signs of developing tolerance for those different from themselves. These events left Alexander with a hopeful feeling.

Yet he was aware that intolerance persisted. He was aware of and concerned about the Iranian government's program to wipe out the Kurds, an indigenous minority, who had remained distinctly different in their beliefs and customs, and had no interest in accepting Iranian culture. As a small but divergent group, they raised goats and sheep, were highly skilled weavers, and lived in isolated northern areas. The Iranian government seemed intent upon wiping out these nomads who refused to pay taxes, live in villages, or accept the Iranian way of life. The efforts to eliminate the Kurds reminded Alexander of other European ethnic holocausts of the past. He wished to express his disapproval of such intolerance. A book set in the Middle East would allow him to "playfully" show what persecution does to a country and suggest how distinct cultures could learn to live together. It would also allow him to develop a message that was more international than those in his earlier stories.

Alexander carefully structured two kinds of intolerance in his plot: the casual intolerance of people towards other people within their own culture and the explicit prejudice against a culture that exists side by side with another. He hoped to show his readers that both were destructive.

Alexander begins his story in an isolated village somewhere in Europe. His main character, an orphan, is harbored by the townspeople. The boy is a notorious snoop and is equally known for his unwillingness to work. The villagers are hard-working peasants, but Lukas is not. He tells the carpenter Nicholas, "I have a terrible ailment. Work makes me ill. Even the word gives me fits."[10] Since Lukas is an orphan with no one to teach him cultural values, he escapes all daily routines other than snooping. He is tolerated by a community that sees him as the village loafer and its particular source of entertainment. The citizens perceive him as different from them and view him as their personal scapegoat.

After establishing that Lukas is different from the other villagers, Alexander introduces a traveling company and shows the town's desire for more worldly entertainment. Like Lukas, the company's leader Battisto the Magnificent, a professional trickster, is different from the villagers. And, he is different from Lukas. The villagers, however, see a link between the two, and, when Battisto asks for a volunteer from the audience, the villagers recommend Lukas. Alexander writes:

> Laughing and hooting, the onlookers pressed Lukas closer to the wagon. He needed no urging, since he enjoyed giving a performance as much as watching one. He

bowed with mock reverence, flexed his arms in a comical
show of brawn, then stood on his hands and kicked his
heels in the air. The crowd whistled and the baker's boy
called out:

"That's right, Lukas-Kasha! Show us where your wits
are. In your feet!"

This brought more laughter and catcalls. Lukas
righted himself, but before he could fling a proper insult
at the baker's dunce, Battisto motioned him to the steps.

Having spent his only coin for entertainment, entertainment there would be, even if Lukas had to provide it
himself. (*Lukas*, 6)

Thus, the two entertainers are linked together. Lukas, the lesser
of the two, becomes Battisto's servant. His daring is exhibited in
his actions. Although he has no idea what Battisto plans, he willingly does as told. Because he is not cautious, he leaves the village
under the magician's spell and travels through time to another
world.

Alexander's subtle contrast between Lukas and the others in
his European town is soon overshadowed by his treatment of Lukas's entrance into a totally foreign country where two alien cultures live side by side, though not in harmony. Time travel is a
central device in *The First Two Lives of Lukas-Kasha* as it was in
Time Cat. However, the talking beasts of *Time Cat* are missing in
The First Two Lives of Lukas-Kasha. Once in another country,
Lukas is not guided by the supernatural. In this second story,
time travel is Alexander's expedient means of getting the book's
youthful male protagonist from one setting to another. It is a way
of taking the reader from the familiar to the unfamiliar. Once in
the unfamiliar, Alexander can expose his young reader to problems deriving from attitudes of ethnic supremacy.

Alexander's story shows how powerful cultures subject lesser
groups to their traditions on the grounds that their attitudes are
more progressive and should be accepted by all. Unwilling to listen to a small group of "natives," these ruling classes determine
that cultural divergence is not acceptable. They seek to create a

melting pot of attitudes by subjecting all to their rules and traditions, hoping ultimately to ingrain their beliefs on all groups.
They do not condone minority opinion. *The First Two Lives of
Lukas-Kasha* is Alexander's first attempt at setting up the message that will dominate his Vesper adventures.

Lukas is washed ashore on a white beach and immediately is
confronted with the reality of his new scene: "The illusion here
was amazing. The sand felt gritty under his feet. The dazzling
sun, the ocean seemed real beyond a doubt. He had even begun
trembling, and it was all he could do to keep his teeth from chat-
tering" (*Lukas,* 9). Soon after, Alexander informs his reader that
"this was no dream" and that Lukas-Kasha cannot be certain Battisto will be able to bring him back to his own village.

Once the reader accepts the premise that Lukas has truly arrived in a foreign country, Alexander changes his style from the
fantasy genre to that of an adventure story. All the adventures in
this land are possible, although they are not always plausible.
The plot is fast paced, and much happens. Alexander's main character becomes involved in palace intrigue, travels across the
country with a political satirist and a female rebel, and works to
resolve a regional conflict between two divergent cultures. The
events contain a number of chance meetings and unplanned situations, and they add to Alexander's sense of fatalism.

All of this could have been placed in two divergent European
cultures, but Alexander's choice of the Middle East as a setting
forces the young Western reader to acknowledge that people who
seem "very foreign" can be understood and appreciated. In addition, it allows Alexander to point out some of the philosophies
that separate the East from the West.

Because Lukas-Kasha has landed in an Islamic land, Alexander can play with the differences between fate and chance. Although Abadan is not specifically labeled a Moslem country, the
people live by some of the Moslem philosophies. One of the important ones is that the fates rule circumstances. Events can be
foretold, but they cannot be changed. Lukas is pursued by horse-
men as soon as the girl rebel disappears, and he is knocked un-
conscious in a fall. When he awakens he finds that he has been

declared the ruler of the country. Upon seeing Lukas, the court astrologer says, "I am delighted to say that your coming has been exactly as I foretold" (*Lukas,* 17).

To Lukas's surprise, the people in this country believe that the future can be predicted but do not believe it can be controlled. When the opposing faction tries to kill Lukas and is unsuccessful, the astrologer Locman tells Lukas, "In all my observations there was not the slightest clue that you were to be assassinated. The Vizier should have had the decency to consult me. I could have assured him his plot was doomed to fail" (*Lukas,* 119). Thus, Alexander shows his reader that the people of Abadan believe in fatalism. If events are meant to happen, they will, regardless of man's plans. But, man can calculate the future by looking at past events and forewarnings of future ones.

Alexander's hero, Lukas, is destined by circumstance to become involved in the struggle between the two cultures. From the moment he lands on the beach, his fate is decided by events beyond his control. When he arrives, he sees a young horseman riding a white horse across the sand. Alexander writes:

> It was a girl, wearing rough cotton trousers and tunic. He put out a hand to catch the bridle, then saw she rode without saddle or harness.
>
> "Tell me," cried Lukas, "Where am I?"
>
> The girl stared for an instant. In her sunburnt face, her yellow eyes glared at him. She spun her mount aside. Without a word, she clapped bare heels against the horse's flanks.
>
> "Wait! Hold on a minute!" Lukas called, as horse and rider plunged away.
>
> "To the devil with you, then," he shouted after the girl, who soon galloped out of sight. (*Lukas,* 11)

This first encounter introduces the book's female protagonist and links her story to Lukas's. They happen to be at the same place when Lukas is washed ashore, and their paths continue to cross.

Throughout their adventures, the girl's fate is also largely determined by circumstances beyond her control.

Alexander uses his female protagonist to contrast the difference between someone who understands how circumstances control the future and someone who wishes to change conditions. Nur-Jehan is aware of her fate, and she accepts her duties as a warring rebel much easier than Lukas accepts his new role of king. A member of Eastern society, she believes that the future is controlled by the past. Lukas has stumbled into something beyond his control. Yet he believes he can effect change. Once in Abadan, the male hero is out of step with his past, but he brings his cultural values with him. He must be willing to learn about other ways in order to bring peace to a foreign culture and return to his European home. There, he can tell others about the merging of two distinct cultures. The heroine, in contrast, must accept her role as the leader of her people and remain in her homeland to rule justly. In the past, Nur-Jehan's people have been unfairly treated; yet, she must teach them to trust their enemies and to work with them if both cultures are going to survive. At the book's end she remains within the confines of her culture, remembering what she has learned while living with another group of people. Although parallel, the journeys of these two characters are different.

Like many other heroines in Alexander's stories, this native girl is not impressed by the book's male hero. Unlike Alexander's earlier heroine in the Prydain series, Nur-Jehan does not prattle or attempt to help the hero. Of the two heroes in *The First Two Lives of Lukas Kasha*, she is the more mysterious, and, as the story develops, she will be seen as the more self-assured. She is depicted as a strong-willed young woman who is determined to return to her people and help in the ensuing war. Nur-Jehan is a defiant warrior, the ruler of her people, the hidden queen who has designed the strategy followed in the rebel attempts to remain free. She is similar to the later Westmark series's beggar queen in several ways, and she may be an early prototype of Alexander's later, more heroic reluctant ruler, Mickle.

At first, Lukas agrees to be king to save himself from death. He also assumes he will like the lazy life of a king. He discovers, however, that the army leader and grand vizier plan to destroy all of the Bishangari because they are "brigands" who allow women to sit at the council table and do not understand the material wealth of their lands, and he determines to become a dominant power within his court's council. Lukas acts to stop bigotry.

Alexander shows his reader that only a knowledgeable leader who is aware of a country's customs and willing to take chances can cause change. Lukas is not familiar with the laws of Abadan; he cannot answer his council's questions. Humiliated by his lack of knowledge, he begins to read and finds criminal punishments he considers unjust. When he asks Locman how he can change the law, he is told that it takes several years to rewrite laws. Later, he meets Nur-Jehan in the gardens, and she warns him to quit meddling with state affairs, saying, "Go too far, overstep yourself, they will not support you. . . . Your efforts are in vain. If you insist on making them, beware" (*Lukas,* 43). Once he attends the Divan of Judgment, he is forced into action. A versifier who speaks out against the government has been sentenced to have his tongue torn out before he is killed. The Grand Vizier Shugdad tells Lukas that the sentence is written and must be carried out. Lukas revokes the sentence and warns, "If you condemn everyone who makes fun of you, that might depopulate the kingdom" (*Lukas,* 46). When the sentence is lifted, he is forced to take the versifier on as his personal servant. Thus, a rebel becomes his closest aide and he becomes a thorn in the council's side.

Alexander has set Lukas-Kasha up in the middle of a cultural conflict between a nomadic minority and a ruling class within the first quarter of the book. Lukas-Kasha, Nur-Jehan, and the condemned versifier Kayim come to the Abadan court from the outside, representing minority opinion and beliefs. Although allies, they misunderstand one another. Nur-Jehan is scornful of Lukas-Kasha and his overtures of help. She asks, "Why does the King act on behalf of his enemy?" and is told, "The whole business is stupid. Both sides will end up killing each other" (*Lukas,* 41). Later, when they have escaped from the palace and are fleeing, Nur-Jehan leads them across the mountains. Her pace bothers both men, and Kayim describes her as half cat and half goat. Lukas says, "She's a stringy, prickly, hot-blooded village vixen—but, I swear, she could have ruled the kingdom better than I did" (*Lukas*, 80). As they travel together, the three begin to understand each other. When Nur-Jehan leaves, taking Lukas's dagger, and Kayim observes, "sounds like you've gone and fallen in love with her," Lukas replies, "Worse. . . . I liked her" (*Lukas*, 106).

Like Alexander's beggar queen, Mickle, in *The Kestrel*, Nur-Jehan disappears for the middle third of the book. Yet since Nur-Jehan has not been established as a sympathetic heroine, the loss is less certain. Readers have grown to like and admire Nur-Jehan, but have watched her fight against Lukas's advice and offers of help. Like many people who come from a minority, Nur-Jehan does not seem to trust anyone. She remains secretive about her people, reluctant to share information. Although Alexander implies that Nur-Jehan is trustworthy, he depicts her as revengeful and quick-tempered. Her people's plight has caused her to distrust everyone, to continually pick fights with those she feels do not respect her. Alexander has not convinced his reader that Nur-Jehan is a person who can easily work with others. Instead, he has developed a wild, passionate girl who prefers street fights to debate. She considers Lukas's ability to barter people out of goods an insult to bravery. Prior to her disappearance, however, Nur-Jehan finally admits that, while Lukas's efforts are not always noble, they are prudent. Thus, Alexander has her admit to a change in attitude and shows that both young protagonists learn from one another. Lukas-Kasha learns how to lead people, and Nur-Jehan learns how to be more open with others.

Alexander continually develops the idea that communication causes people to change. In the beginning of the story Lukas serves as the village crier. He tells others the news and draws caricatures of the mayor. Once in Abadan, Lukas seems unable to communicate with the townspeople. As king, he is not allowed in the marketplace. His only friend in the palace is the astrologer Locman. One of his few means to news is Kayim's satirical rhymes, which contain political gossip. He is forced to rely on the reports of others concerning his people. When he and Kayim disappear to the marketplace and try to bargain away some goods, Lukas-Kasha's European talents fail him. Yet, the resulting nosebleed allows him to gossip with a water merchant and to discover that the people like his rule.

The early problems between Lukas-Kasha, Kayim, and Nur-Jehan come when none of the three is effectively listening to the others. When she listens, Nur-Jehan learns that Lukas-Kasha has been sent to Abadan against his will and that he has no idea when, or if, he will ever leave. This gives her new respect for Lukas-Kasha, and she asserts, "Yet you risked your life for the sake of Bishangar, a land that can mean nothing to you" (*Lukas*, 82). Lukas-Kasha reminds her that peace with Bishangar would have been good for Abadan also, and the two reach a new understanding about political truces.

All three protagonists learn to accept each other when they share their ideas and pasts. Kayim and Nur-Jehan begin to banter and jest as they travel across the mountains, and Lukas tells stories of his deeds in Zara-Petra to entertain the others. The spoken word becomes a central tool. Lukas-Kasha tricks a horse thief by telling him an outrageous tale, and both Lukas-Kasha and Kayim choose storytelling when they turn to "a very painful prospect, honest work" (*Lukas*, 107).

Stories also help the minor characters. The astrologer comes up with a new method of predicting the future by telling parables, and the water merchant who earlier gossiped with Lukas-Kasha turns up twice to save Kayim and Lukas-Kasha by misleading their enemies with his directions and his storytelling stance. Lukas frees the country from its band of cutthroat bandits by creating a story of deceit and spreading distrust among the band's leaders. Lukas and Kayim save a young Bishangari lad who talks continually. Once in a village of the Bishangari, the two discover that even the children are good storytellers. In the end Lukas learns that Nur-Jehan's father, King Ardashir, has been dead for years, but that tales of his deeds as a guerrilla warrior have kept him alive for the people of Abadan.

Alexander weaves his plot together with a bag of stories, each cleverly developed and told. Alexander implies with his careful manipulation of storytelling that humor and the ability to laugh at oneself are qualities that are important to all people. He also suggests that storytellers need receptive listeners.

Unlike some of Alexander's earlier books, there is little bloodshed in the plot. When Lukas's deeds do cause the death of the villain Shugdad, he doubts that he has successfully won the battle. Alexander writes:

> Lukas glimpsed what Osman had held aloft by the hair. He turned his eyes away, stomach heaving. He heard voices shouting his name. Nur-Jehan was galloping toward him, Kayim beside her. It took some moments before he understood what they were telling him.
> "Won?" murmured Lukas. "Yes, I suppose we have." (*Lukas,* 195)

Lukas is out of step with war. He is a peacemaker who depends upon storytelling and compromise. He wants to change attitudes without losing lives.

Thus Alexander has broken away from his earlier fantasy tradition. He has begun to consider how political ideas and attitudes can be "playfully treated" within books meant for a young readership. When Alexander wrote about the playfulness in fantasy he added "and art in general," implying that all genres demanded the author's careful manipulation of events, character, and settings if he hopes to develop a philosophical stance within the story. Alexander's next books would show that he was becoming more concerned with writing for a slightly older audience. These stories would contain his then current attitudes about society and would subtly shape themes of idealism for future generations.

7

Another Country: The Westmark Series

When children's literature expert Jean Greenlaw asked Alexander what genre the Westmark series, a trilogy, fits into, he responded, "The only way I could manage to express myself was through that particular kind of story which oddly enough turned out not to be a fantasy in the sense that there is no magic in it, there's no enchantment, there's no magical spells. . . . It's a fantasy to the extent that it never happened. It takes place somewhere that never existed in a world that never existed. . . . But, it could happen in real life, presumably."[1]

Typically, fantasy writers consciously break with the realities of the everyday world. They mold a world that seems real but contains elements not found in ordinary situations. Conventional devices, characters, and symbols found in folklore are often employed. The authors of children's fantasies often combine a whimsical tone with the trappings of the bildungsroman plot to create stories that seem to be both lighthearted and philosophical. They construct plots and characters for an audience with certain expectations. Although early children's fantasies contained stories that were largely religious allegories, more recent children's writers have often concentrated upon the political or social aspects of society.

But the Westmark series' emphasis on historical, sociological and political ideologies suggests that the adventures do not fit into the structural motifs of traditional fantasy. The ideas examined are more closely linked with past known worldwide struggles of revolt and revolution, and they showcase conflicting ideas about what reflects good political leadership and government. Unburdened with the traditional trappings of fantasy, the Westmark characters go beyond the typical heroic questing pattern and enter into the dark sides of political upheaval. Although the stories are set in a nonexistent country, the series contains personalities who resemble personages from the world's past. By no means fantastic themselves, they do not resort to supernatural or magical solutions.

Set in a fabricated country, the Westmark series deals with the realities of political events more than Alexander's earlier fantasies. He had always been concerned with governmental struggles and had written books that emphasized the virtues of humane leadership. However, Alexander had never concentrated on political power's ability to corrupt. His earlier heroes had grown in stature as they experienced adventures, remaining pure of both mind and heart. His earlier books stressed the hero's difficulties when leading others within battle and his need to sacrifice his personal desire for glory in order to create a stable, and ultimately democratic, society.

The Tragic Hero

In Alexander's fantasies his youthful heroes had no psychological dark sides. In contrast, the male protagonist of the Westmark series, Theo, is at times driven by his dark side, and, when he is involved in the horrors of war, his actions are less than heroic. Although he faces the challenges of idealism, he is more vulnerable in his reactions. Thus he plots vengeance for his enemies and stoops to unheroic actions. As he matures, he is forced to recognize that his ruthlessness has driven him beyond justice. Theo becomes a tragic hero, burdened with self-doubts and character flaws that inflame his actions during the country's political strife.

By the second book in the series Theo is an established leader.

He is not struggling for power; it is his already. Instead, he is struggling against factions that hope to overthrow the government. And he is struggling with himself and some of his youthful comrades who are driven by personal revenge and hatred more than by idealistic goals. As the series evolves, Alexander depicts some of the young characters as radicals driven by a cause, people who make good wartime leaders, but lack the compassion and wisdom needed during times of peace. These characters show that war does not always bring out the best in humanity, that it fosters behavior that must not dominate in peace. They demonstrate that leaders driven by personal values will sometimes depend upon intrigue and deceit to gain their goals, that they will sacrifice the safety of those who serve them for their own purposes.

Alexander's Westmark males are sometimes driven by personal desires and prejudices. Furthermore, they come from richly diverse backgrounds and illustrate that events are shaped by many types of characters, not by one antagonist and protagonist. The diversity in characters and in the subplots that bring their individual dramas alive emphasizes the role that fate has played in shaping history.

Alexander did a good deal of reading, mostly about the French Revolution, prior to his writing. Once the series was completed Alexander wrote,

> It would be misleading to suggest parallels between real history and the history of people who never existed except in the kingdom of Westmark. Still, everything comes from something, and behind my imagined characters are vague shadows of historical figures.
>
> For example: the notorious eighteenth century charlatan, Joseph Balsamo, known as Cagliostro. While there is no spiritual kinship between this semi-criminal and my exuberant, good-hearted mountebank, my private amusement was to use anagrams of "Balsamo" for Count Las Bombas and his numerous aliases.
>
> And there are other instances. Lurking behind Keller, the journalist, I catch a fleeting glimpse of Jacques-Rene

Hebert, publisher of the satirical newspaper, *Pere Du-
chesne*. As for the implacable revolutionary, Justin, there
are threads connecting him with Louis Antoine de St.
Just, one of the leaders of the Reign of Terror. Young,
strikingly handsome, he was described by his contemporaries as being beautiful as an angel, but so merciless
and bloodthirsty that he was nicknamed "the Angel of
Death."

Looking at the portrait of a young officer, lean-fea-
tured, long hair and loose, I can see, superimposed,
the face of the gallant and charismatic Florian. (The
subject of the original portrait was named Napoleon
Bonaparte.)[2]

Although the adventures do happen in an imaginary world,
they have much to do with the French Revolution and with the
twentieth century. The two eras are similar in the lack of moral
political leadership.

The talks and commentary given while Alexander was writing
the series affirm that he was thinking of something different from
fantasy, something that would appeal to a new audience. As he
spoke, he mentioned Dickens, Shakespeare, and Mark Twain. All
three wrote books with barbed social commentary. They penned
in rogues and outcasts, and they placed controversial ideas in
seemingly straightforward narratives. Their writing styles allowed them to comment on society within the context of an adventure story. Alexander admired their storytelling, and, whether
it was an accident or a conscious decision, he left behind traditional fantasy conventions and emulated these earlier masters in
a series that could be likened in plot to Tolstoy's *War and Peace*
with its "cast of thousands" carefully interconnected in a intri-
cately designed plot and tied together within several episodic
adventures.

The Westmark series's tone and events point it toward a more
mature audience, one aware of the world around it, a high school
rather than an elementary school readership. Alexander's readers
might already be questioning corruption in political leadership.

The youths who read the series may even be considering what role they can take in shaping their country's destiny. They are beginning to determine how their moral and political beliefs relate to their personal goals.

Throughout the story, Alexander deals with the problems of ineffectual leadership. Much like a Marxist, he suggests that corrupt government will result in an upheaval of power and will return it to the proletariat. A true believer in democracy who is aware of the bloody consequences of the French Revolution, Alexander uses this series to warn that all shifts in leadership can lead to factional conflict. He contrasts compassion with strength and shows how moral weakness breeds political intrigue and corruption. Alexander breaks from his earlier romantic style and replaces it with realism.

Political Commentary

The modern reader who enters into the kingdom of Westmark does not enter into a country that is foreign from the realities of the world today. Although the country is ruled by a king, he might be replaced by any weak and ineffectual leader. The people who inhabit the adventures resemble real-life characters of the past.

Alexander had seen Hitler rise to power and manipulate the common people's values. He was aware of America's twentieth-century attitudes of superiority and complacency. He had seen Klansmen stir up racial and religious hatred and had watched his country's leaders take the American people into wars designed to "free the world from the threat of communism." Alexander distrusted America's political right. Written at a time when Jimmy Carter was being replaced by Ronald Reagan, the Westmark series is a warning to young people against paternalistic and autocratic rulers.

This is Alexander's strong personal statement concerning war, democracy, personal integrity, and social protest, largely based on his own readings and experiences. The narrative alludes to history and suggests that any new governmental system should be nurtured with attitudes of justice and fairness. In the Westmark books Alexander tells a story that ties the past to the present, both as an interpretation of history and the literary structures of the political and historical novel.

Westmark

Westmark, the first book of the series, combines several stories in one plot. The book is broken into four parts, each with its own subtitle. They are "The Printer's Devil," "The Oracle Priestess," "Florian's Children," and "The Garden of Cabbarus." The subtitles pinpoint the major characters in the story and reflect their roles in drama. They signal that Theo's importance rests in his understanding of the press and its role in government, that Mickle has a secret that she herself is not aware of, that Florian is a fatherly leader for the revolting masses, and that Cabbarus's intrigue lies in the palace.

The book's early adventures resemble the picaresque novel. The plot is highly episodic, jumping from one set of characters to another. Theo and Mickle tie the adventures together, becoming unlikely compatriots in the country's political struggle. Alexander uses Theo's and Mickle's adventures to show that corrupt leadership can cause political intrigue and revolution. The villain Cabbarus's injustices and the king's ineffective leadership cause the young characters to act without forethought. In the end, Alexander weaves together all of the book's subplots, combining the political with the romantic and picaresque.

Westmark has an extremely large cast of characters and is set in numerous locations. The reader must be able to follow several shifts in scenes, trusting that the author's multitude of characters and scenes will ultimately merge into a central story. The multi-layered plot structure is suited for a reader experienced with literary conventions. Its continuity depends upon certain stock characters who maintain their attitudes and behaviors throughout. Thus, Las Bombas remains a *picaro,* Cabbarus is always depicted as a villain, the king is constantly ineffective, and Dr. Torrens becomes the symbolic idealist.

Alexander wins his readers in the beginning by presenting favorable adolescent characters. Realizing that the young reader's focus is primarily placed on this youthful cast of characters, Alexander introduces them while he sets the tone for the series and he establishes that this is not fantasy.

Alexander begins by telling his reader that "Theo, by occupation was a devil." Then he explains that Theo is a printer's apprentice and goes on to state "before that, he was lucky enough to be an orphan, for the town fathers of Dorning prided themselves in looking after their needy." The reader is told that Theo was "made miserable" locally until he accidentally learned to read and was considered "spoiled . . . for anything sensible."[3] Alexander's use of irony in his opening paragraph signals that he is writing for an older audience, and his description of the young hero as one who is happy in his fate and is not seeking adventure suggests that this book will not fit the typical questing pattern.

Theo is portrayed as an interesting and likable young man, but he has no drive to become a hero. Alexander states, "As for Theo, he loved virtue, despised injustice, and was always slightly hungry. Apart from that, he was reasonably happy" (*Westmark,* 10).

Within the first chapter Alexander forces Theo into an adventure and captures the reader with the story of political upheaval. In Theo's journey away from his provincial town he encounters the other youthful protagonists, becomes involved in theatrics and politics, helps Mickle find her place as the missing princess, and takes a job as a counselor for the court.

In the first chapter Alexander indirectly introduces the series' political villain. The printing trade is suffering, the reader is told, because the Chief Minister Cabbarus "eyed [every publication] with suspicion" (*Westmark,* 10). Alexander then uses a physical break in the narrative to graphically note a change of pace and begins the next paragraph by having one of the rogues, Musket, come striding into the printing shop. This is Alexander's most "fantastic" character in his series. Musket is described as a dwarf. Alexander, however, does not give him a supernatural aura. He is physically different, but he is not a fantasy personality. His swaggering entrance and curt ways give him a sense of authority and his quick actions set Alexander's pace. Musket asks if Theo, whose master is out of the shop, can get a printing job done for him by the first thing the next day, and Theo agrees to take on the job. Theo becomes a rebel by defying the law and taking on Musket's unsanctioned job. The outcome of his defiance is quickly apparent. In a rapid succession of events, Theo's master returns, Cabbarus is discussed by the two as a scoundrel who is stopping freedom of the press, the job for Musket is perfected, government officers arrive to destroy the press, Theo attacks the commanding officer, and Theo's master is killed. By the end of the first sixteen pages Theo is a wanted criminal, fleeing from the king's soldiers.

At this point Theo's development of an inner conflict between what is right and wrong is secondary to his adventures. So far, he has not been pictured as idealistic. He has bent the law by taking a printing job without getting the proper permit; he quickly acted in his master's defense, further compounding his crime. Hotheaded and naive, he has unintentionally become a rebel. As the central character in all three of the books, he represents the country's common citizens.

By moving Theo away from Dorning to the highways of the kingdom, Alexander has set the stage for his picaresque story. His two *picaros,* Musket and Las Bombas, appear, and the story takes on a lighter mood. Although Musket and Las Bombas have volatile personalities, they do not use weapons. Instead, they thrive on deceit. Las Bombas saves Theo from the military by having him act like a wild savage. Once Theo is saved, he quickly learns that to survive he must alter some of his sense of morality. He understands that he is involved in harmless scams, that his fellow rogues do not want to physically harm anyone or to gain control over anyone's destiny. Thus, Alexander implies that poor men who must resort to deceit use dishonesty in different ways from those who are wealthy. Musket explains that half of the beggars in the country have been "custom-tailored for the trade. Youngsters bought or stolen, then broken past mending. . . . Sold off to a master who pockets whatever charity's thrown to them." Musket tells Theo that Las Bombas is a good-natured rascal who does not hurt others. He reminds Theo that the rich are deceptively ruthless, saying, "Take your nobles who flog their servants, gouge their tenants, or the judges who send some wretch to be hanged—they're honest as the day is long. Any scoundrel can be honest." Musket suggests that Las Bombas is a charlatan because "he can't stomach the world as he finds it" and asks Theo, "Can You?" (*Westmark,* 46).

Throughout the book Alexander toys with the idea that there are different kinds of scoundrels. These two are rogues, but they are sympathetically portrayed. Their deception harms no one, and it helps to make the world around them a more entertaining place. Although Alexander implies that some scoundrels are more acceptable than others, he does not have Theo come directly to this conclusion. The meanings of deception and honor are left up to the reader.

Once Theo is outlawed, his destiny is structured by fate. His story becomes highly adventurous, more loosely constructed. At the same time, Alexander begins to weave in a second plot and to develop a story of political unrest, a story that contrasts with Theo's because its main character wants to control destiny. Alexander turns to the castle and the cast of characters within the government. While Theo is left traveling the road in Tom Jones fashion, the reader is introduced to Cabbarus and his plot to overthrow the king and rule the country.

Castle Intrigue

Introduced in the fifth chapter of *Westmark,* Alexander's castle intrigue at first seems to have little to do with the earlier episodes. Throughout the first four chapters, however, the reader has been cautioned that a second story will appear. Alexander has established that the unrest seen in the country is the result of poor leadership. Cabbarus has been mentioned by the fifth page of the book and implicated as the villain, so the reader anticipates his appearance in the story. From Alexander's casual remarks the reader understands that if Cabbarus rules, the country will be changed.

Cabbarus is portrayed as a stereotypical villain. He is an overly ambitious governmental worker who has always been willing to take on all of the tasks everyone else finds too boring. This ruthless politician now controls the entire workings of the government. Although he could live luxuriously, he prefers to live frugally. As an aspiring despot with a high opinion of himself, Cabbarus does not seek wealth. He believes he is more fit to rule than the country's king. He is vain and egocentric. There is no reason to suspect that he has any compassion. His desire to execute the printers who "cause nothing but unrest" (*Westmark*, 36) is a catalyst for rebellion.

Cabbarus is the story's villain, but no one in the government is faultless. Alexander has linked his two stories with sporadic details about the disappearance of the King Augustine's only heir, a daughter. Once inside the castle, the reader discovers that the king has been immobilized with grief over his daughter's disappearance, and the other ministers are afraid to act without Cabbarus's approval. The king's loss of control in this decaying monarchy causes the political uneasiness. When Cabbarus enters the ailing king's dismal quarters to beg for the right to rule, the reader realizes that change will follow. Cabbarus cannot stomach freethinking, freewheeling individuals. Cabbarus's idea that he be declared the successor to the throne causes the king's ailing health to crumble, and both the reader and the king are unsettled.

The hero within the castle, Dr. Torrens, the king's loyal physician, is described as a man with a blunt, broad face whose unpowdered hair has been tied back by "a common bow" (*Westmark*, 40). Torrens's coarse features contrast with Cabbarus's miserly appearance. Unlike Cabbarus, who feeds on the king's sadness, he argues that the king's health will best be remedied with good food, sleep, and fresh air, setting up a confrontation between natural goodness and deceit. Torrens understands the king's grief at the loss of his only child. But he remains strong in his conviction that the king must shake off his despair and rule his country. Like the peasants in the villages, Torrens is aware that the country needs a strong leader who seeks the good of the people. As an intermediary for the kingdom, he has been able to stop the wicked Cabbarus until now.

As the castle scene develops, the reader is aware that Cabbarus is not accepted as the king's heir by everyone. The queen sides with Torrens in her opposition to Cabbarus. At the end of the fifth chapter Dr. Torrens calls Cabbarus a scoundrel. Cabbarus plans retaliation and remarks to himself, "As for Torrens, he would be dealt with. A plan was already shaping in his mind. It always pleased the chief minister how clear-sighted he could be in clouded circumstances" (*Westmark,* 42).

The story unfolding in the castle is tied to the outside world by the disappearance of the princess and the king's inability to cope. The outside world is tied to the government by Cabbarus's attempts to control. The plots begin to merge when Cabbarus forces Torrens out of the capital city.

In chapter nine, when Torrens implores the king to forget his lost daughter and begin to act like a ruler, the king forfeits his power:

> "Your Highness, do you hear the fellow?" Cabbarus recoiled in shock and indignation. "The truth at last. He admits it. He works against you. A loyal subject would only seek to reunite you and the princess, however briefly. What, then, are we to think of one who desires the opposite?"
>
> Cabbarus stretched out an accusing finger at the court physician. "You have gone too far. You are dismissed from His Majesty's service. Banished from the kingdom. Return at your peril, under the pain of death. Be grateful your punishment is so light."
>
> "These are your words, not the king's. You have done your best to make a puppet of him, and have done all too well . . . I beg you, Sire, listen to me. You risk your life and sanity for no purpose. This villain puts words in your mouth. Speak for yourself."
>
> Augustine's lips trembled, but the words were clear. "We banish you. Set foot in our kingdom and your life is forfeit. Such is our Royal Will." (*Westmark,* 66)

Torrens is last seen three pages later facing an assassin. Thus Alexander concludes the section with this cliffhanger and returns the drama to the countryside and Theo in order to establish him as the real hero of *Westmark.*

Theo displays uneasiness with his new life with Las Bombas and Musket. He cannot accept their trickery and misrepresentation as honorable behavior. Nevertheless, Theo does not act until the heroine Mickle and a sense of romance is introduced. When Mickle appears, Theo is protective of the young girl and resents Las Bombas's scheme to use her as an oracle priestess. He finally acknowledges that innocent people are being hurt by the troupe's deceptions and parts company with the traveling band of rogues while all are asleep.

If Theo represents a person with an evolving sense of social moralism, Mickle represents the rogue in society. Alexander describes her as a street urchin who is "a collection of skin and bones." He goes on to add, "She wore a pair of ragged breeches tied with a rope about her bony hips, and a dirty shirt with more holes than cloth. She was drab as a street sparrow, with a beaky nose in a narrow face. Her eyes were blue, but pale as if the color had been starved out of them" (*Westmark,* 53–54).

Mickle is a streetwise youth who has never known the security of a home. She knows little of her past and is uncomfortable with her ignorance. She remembers only being raised by a burglar who was caught working in his trade and hung for his efforts. When Las Bombas suggests that she join them in their pursuits, Theo objects that she is not a stray cat to be picked up off the streets. The girl immediately shows that she is used to making her living and is capable of making her own decisions by putting Theo down. Thus Alexander establishes Mickle as a waif who can fend for herself but who is insecure with her lot in life.

Mickle fits into the picaresque lives of Las Bombas and Musket. She is a trickster who enjoys doing her fraudulent performances. The fact that she turns out to be the kingdom's missing princess who must leave her life of crime in order to learn to rule solidifies the book as a picaresque novel.

Alexander's social commentary comes into sharper play after Theo abandons the traveling company. At this point, Alexander introduces a third set of characters and turns his attention to the realities of revolution by introducing a group of political rebels. These are Alexander's representations from history.

The leader of these youthful rebels, Florian, is a mysterious young man who "seemed to have crossed some invisible line giving him authority beyond the number of his birthdays." This romantic rebel is poetically described: "His hair was light brown and he wore it long and loose. Pockmarks sprayed his cheeks and the bridge of his finely drawn nose. He was studying Theo with apparently idle amusement; but his gray eyes took in everything at once, observing, calculating, and summing up the result" (*Westmark,* 89). The young man's physical appearance marks him as a hero. He is a charismatic leader, outspoken concerning the government's sins, and worshiped by his youthful followers.

Theo remains with Florian and works as a scribe for the villagers, learning that commoners are suffering vast injustices under the present government. Drawn into the political activity of the rebels, Theo almost forgets about the rogues he left behind. Thus, Alexander points out how easy it is for young people to forget their pasts when introduced to new ideas and associates.

Halfway through the book Alexander merges the divergent casts of characters and introduces the last set of important characters. These characters add new dimensions to the overall story. Through them, Alexander adds another political dimension to his story. Although they are basically nameless, they represent the large number of poor who combine forces with idealists during revolutionary times. Their movements can help to make a revolution successful.

By having some of his earlier characters become involved in the country's unrest by chance, Alexander emphasizes that attachment of any group with another during unrest and the resulting collaboration of various factions are sometimes results of unforeseen circumstances. For instance, the pair of urchins who happen upon Dr. Torrens when he reappears are not aware that their lives will be changed by this chance event. Sparrow and Weasel, sister and brother "water rats," fend for themselves by taking "pickings" cast into the city's muddy swampland. In Dickensian style, these children harvest the pockets of dead bodies. They fish Torrens out of the marshy waters in The Fingers to rob his pockets. However, Torrens is alive, and they take him to their crude home where Alexander introduces another new character, a lanky young man with chestnut hair and a pale face. Although the young man is actually Keller, a journalist, he is known as "Old Kasperl," the renegade political commentator. Earlier, his editorials had caused him to be cast into prison. He, too, has escaped death and is living with the water rats.

Circumstances begin to bring various characters together. Keller has heard about Florian and his band, and he proposes that he and Torrens venture into the countryside to find them. In the meantime, Theo has learned that Las Bombas, Musket, and Mickle have been arrested for their deceit, and he goes to the town of Nierkeeping with Florian and a group of his followers to free them. Florian leads the band to the hideout of a group of countryside resistance fighters who will raid the town and help Theo free his friends. And so, Alexander's factions are brought together through a series of chance meetings.

Because the adventures seem disjointed, Alexander is able to switch from one scene to another, from one set of characters and their motives to another, without losing his reader's interest. Within the loose episodic framework Alexander shifts his story from the adventures of the common people back to the political intrigue of the castle. Once the link between the characters and subplots is established, however, Alexander breaks with his early picaresque style and creates a more serious story that contains a romance in the strict sense. Political intrigue becomes a focal part of his story, and he changes his tone. Thus Alexander begins to deal with the problems of political unrest in a more serious manner, revealing the ensuing military clashes and their outcomes. With the final interweaving of the plot's central characters, the action shifts to Alexander's central theme that weak and unscrupulous leaders will cause political unrest and intrigue that can spur revolutionary activities.

Alexander's central figures express diverging ideologies during the last third of the book. Theo reacts to the earlier fight in his master's printing shop by becoming a pacifist. Torrens wishes to free the monarchy of Cabbarus and joins with the rebel forces. Florian wishes to overthrow the monarchy and chooses to lead his followers into an open confrontation. Ultimately, governmental change comes when the conflicting ideologies join forces, forsaking personal goals and ideals for a common cause. However, Alexander ends *Westmark* by revealing that the individual goals of the various factions have not been replaced. Torrens remains a monarchist, and Florian a revolutionary. During his first military battle Theo remembers his past and is unable to kill another man and save Justin, a comrade-in-arms, from injury. He must be saved from humiliation by Florian. At the book's end, Theo pursues the villain Cabbarus to a tower, struggles with him, and saves him from falling to his death. Theo's two pacifist actions will haunt him throughout the series. And Theo remains divided between the monarchy and the rebels. Mickle is now a princess, but Theo's loyalties to Florian remain strong.

Once peace is restored and Mickle is declared a princess, the book quickly winds down. Torrens is appointed prime minister, Las Bombas and Musket are rewarded for their part in returning the princess to the king, Florian and his friends disperse, and Theo is sent out of the capital city to be the government's envoy, while Mickle is to stay behind and learn the ways of royalty.

Alexander ends the story without changing Mickle's personality. She is wealthy now, but any change is largely external rather than internal. In the last paragraph of the book the willful Mickle rebuffs her ladies-in-waiting by sticking her tongue out at them when they inform her that she must return to the castle. Then she uses her street sign language to tell Theo, "Find what you want. I will find you" (*Westmark*, 190).

Westmark is the most entertaining book in the series. Although it begins to deal with the problems of corrupt government, it does not contain the sting that will be delivered in the final two books. It reads like traditional children's literature. The plot is full of intrigue and adventure. Although the "fairy tale" romance is secondary, it is obvious. Had Alexander not carefully placed Theo's inability to determine his philosophy concerning governmental rule and social insurrection within the adventure, the drama might have ended. As it stands, the adventure is incomplete by itself. Within the second volume the horrors of circumstances and of wartime are evident.

The Kestrel

Like *Westmark*, its sequel, *The Kestrel*, is divided into distinct parts. The three subdivisions signify the psychological effects of the war. The characterization is established, and the subplots are set up in the format. Although the book may seem like *Westmark* at this point, it is very different in style and construction. It is more somber than *Westmark*, and it begins with a flashback rather than an adventurous scene.

The first segment, "The Beggar Queen," immediately begins to set up the ensuing political intrigue and the war. The second segment, "The Monkey," depicts Theo's corruption. The final third of the book, "The Kestrel," relates Theo's obvious lack of concern for his fellow man during the peak of his military career. Thus, Theo becomes a tragic hero, and the book becomes more somber in tone and implied message.

The Kestrel is not a book that stands on its own. In the first section Alexander's main characters are treated like old friends. The story starts where it left off in *Westmark*, without introductions of characters or explanations of their relationships. The reader of *Westmark* must remember that Theo has been sent to inspect the provinces, since the action begins in the first chapter with Theo on the road. On the first page, he meets Luther, one of the revolutionaries. All of the young revolutionaries are recalled by Theo, and Luther tells him that they are as they were when last seen. Theo relives his moment of terror during the past uprising when he had failed to save Justin from harm, and he anguishes over his cowardice in battle. Thus Alexander has reestablished Theo's divided loyalties. He is the crown's servant, but his heart belongs to the revolutionaries. Theo's memory of Justin's injury during the earlier battle points to Theo's personal dilemma of choosing between passivism and fighting during wartime. Throughout the book, Alexander makes it clear that Theo's past haunts him.

Alexander begins to build his conflict between the established government and the young revolutionaries when Luther tells Theo that Florian wants the monarchy to replace Erzcour, a leading general, who is rumored to be plotting against the king. However, the conflict between the rebels and the monarchy does not erupt until the last third of the book. Instead, Theo learns that the king has died and that Mickle is the country's new ruler, and he leaves the inn to travel to the castle.

Once again, Alexander wants to develop several scenes at once, and so he has Theo meet Skeit, the spy who earlier worked for Cabbarus. The villain draws a pistol and shoots, leaving Theo's fate hanging. Immediately, Alexander changes the scene to the castle. He begins,

> Queen Mickle urgently needed a few handfuls of dirt. She had not, until tonight, realized how scarce it was. Her apartments had, as always, been swept and dusted relentlessly.
>
> Her need had sprung up suddenly at the end of the day. That morning, when Dr. Torrens, her chief minister, arrived still without word of Theo, Mickle's patience, even then, was scraped to the bone.[4]

Unlike Theo, who must face up to his dark side, Mickle will remain a heroine throughout the story. Alexander quickly establishes this by describing her appearance to his audience.

In *The Kestrel* Alexander creates visual character sketches for many of his main characters. Designed to support the characters' emotional and moral identity, these portraits create a visual impression that reinforces the characters as symbolic personalities. During Torrens's audience with Mickle, for instance, Alexander has Torrens observe her as an unconventional woman when he mentions that she "paced the private audience chamber, hands clenched in the pockets of the breeches she wore in preference to the cumbersome skirts she suffered at grand ceremonials" (*Kestrel*, 13). Her lack of royal mannerisms is then noted by Torrens as he watches her pace the room. Alexander says, "She looked more street sparrow than imperial eagle. Unlike her mother, the new queen was no beauty at first glance" (*Kestrel*, 14). Yet, Torrens observes, she was capable of some regal posturing, and she had an extremely quick mind.

Alexander quickly establishes Mickle as a strong-willed female who will defy her own advisers. Her domain is not in the castle alone. Mickle is aware of the underlying class tension and its implications. She has learned from Theo that a Baron Montmollin has acquired common land until his holdings amount to half of Westmark. The tension between elitism and new idealism emerges. Mickle seeks to restore the land to the commoners, but Torrens urges her to move slowly in her reforms.

Mickle is not the appropriate heroine for a monarchy. As an idealistic and intelligent female interested in the rights of the masses, Mickle is out of step with the castle leadership. She is a "street sparrow" with romantic ties to a commoner, and she is more concerned about Theo's whereabouts than with Montmollin's estates. When she leaves the castle, it is with little thought of how the government will work without her. Torrens, she knows, will rule in her stead.

In contrast, the sixteen-year-old monarch, King Constantine IX, whose country, Regia, will wage war against Westmark, is described as a "bright-haired, slender young man in disheveled hunting garb" who "clattered into the room." Alexander observes that "while the downy beginnings of a moustache had sprouted on his narrow upper lip, he had not yet come into the full strength of his ancestral features that looked so well on gold coins" (*Kestrel*, 31).

Other characters are left to the reader's imagination because they will be torn by inner conflicts and will not maintain one stance or one image. Most prominent of these characters is Theo. He must be judged by the reader; Alexander refuses to create a visual impression of him.

Throughout the story, Alexander uses external circumstances to develop his plot. Three pages after the reader learns that Mickle is planning her escape from the castle, the rogue Las Bombas appears. Penniless once again, he agrees to take the queen with him on a mission to find Theo, and the traveling companions are once again on the road. The reader discovers that Mickle has fled her castle just when opposing military forces strike out.

Alexander establishes that this is a political novel by immediately placing rebels, royalists, and foreign intrigue into his plot and by introducing a plot to overthrow the government. General Erzcour and Baron Montmollin plan to overthrow Mickle and gain control of Westmark, and their different roles in the intrigue are highlighted when Montmollin assures Erzcour, "You are not betraying your kingdom. Nor am I. We are preserving it. The aristocracy is its blood and bone. . . . The aristocracy alone stands above greed and self-interest" (28). He reintroduces *Westmark's* villain Cabbarus. It turns out he is conspiring with King Constantine's forces in Regia.

Although Constantine is not much younger than Mickle, he is depicted as a headstrong child. His portrayal as an insensitive aristocrat brings into question the sensibilities of monarchism. Alexander develops an obvious contrast between the blatantly self-centered attitudes of Constantine and the egalitarian principles of the rebel Florian. Florian is aware of the country's problems and understands the consequences of war. Alexander describes Florian in these romantic terms: "His elegantly drawn face with its scatter of pockmarks was weather beaten, grained with fine lines. Hatless, hair loose and uncropped, he stood with his thumbs in his belt while his grey eyes observed Theo's surprise with amusement" (*Kestrel,* 34). Florian is a quiet, weathered wartime leader with a sense of aristocracy about him. His appearance is casually handsome, and when he sees Theo his stance is friendly, though he is not awed by a servant of the queen.

Florian is Alexander's leading diplomat who understands those in his command. When, for instance, Theo asks about Justin, Florian says he is "an avenging angel" who "should be especially useful—or especially dangerous—to a great many people, and himself into the bargain" (*Kestrel*, 37). Florian sees Justin as a charismatic personality who cares little about those in his command. When Theo asks Florian to help Mickle, he answers that their help will be given if the government will grant "equality of every man and woman in Westmark; they shall be equal before the law, and the law shall be equal before them. The only privilege I accept is the privilege—no, the right—of making a decent life for ourselves. In short, a constitution. I'll not ask my people to die for anything less" (*Kestrel*, 44). Florian is depicted as a man aware of social values, injustices, and the powers of wealth. By the end of the book the reader learns that Florian's father is the aristocratic Baron Montmollin who earlier plotted against Mickle's rule. Florian resolves to make public amends for his upbringing by disinheriting his past.

Justin represents the renegade commander in war. When he appears in *The Kestrel*, he is described as a guerrilla fighter rather than a traditional soldier. He has "a blanket roll over his shoulder, a pistol in his belt" (*Kestrel*, 39). His hair is bleached from the sun, and his complexion is "weathered to a dark gold." In contrast, the scar caused by Theo's inability to shoot an enemy soldier has become "a stark white furrow" that twists from his brow to his cheek (*Kestrel*, 40). Justin greets Theo as a long lost comrade, and comments about the fateful day when his face was scarred, saying, "'What a glorius day that was, eh? I'll never forget it. My first glorious battle, a real baptism of fire. Yours, too, I think. We were hard pressed, all of us.' Justin lowered his voice as if sharing a secret. 'I can tell you, I thought it was touch and go for a time. Lucky I was on hand to save you from that officer'" (*Kestrel*, 40).

Alexander has depicted three very different wartime leaders with different attitudes. Theo is the government's man, but he is also in sympathy with the rebels. He remembers his earlier "cowardice" and seems determined to act differently in this uprising. Florian is the seasoned leader who wishes to protect his followers from undue dangers but who is willing to put their lives on the line for democracy. Justin is a romantic warrior who enjoys the sights and sounds of battle. He glorifies his wartime past and paints heroic scenes out of his memories. His charm allows him to distort the past. These characters illustrate the conflict between war as an honorable occupation and war as a means to gain personal victories, with Theo holding the middle ground, a place he will hold throughout the book.

Alexander introduces a murderer and soldier of fortune in the Monkey. Described as "a lanky trooper with a wide, snaggle-toothed grin," the Monkey is ill shaven and misformed. He has earned his nickname from his comrades because of his long arms and sloping shoulders. Concerning the ways of war, Alexander notes, "Nothing was beyond the Monkey's skill" (*Kestrel,* 64). The reader hears indirectly that the Monkey has probably been a part of the regular army and that no one cares to learn why he is now a renegade. As Stock, the poet of the guerrilla troop says, "Who cares? He's a gem. Justin's lucky to have him" (*Kestrel,* 65). Alexander introduces the Monkey to show that war is not always honorable.

Once the Monkey is established as a stigma of war mentality, the second section of the book begins. As the story progresses, the reader learns that the Monkey steals rations from the villagers, tortures and kills enemy soldiers, and creates his own rules to live by. Alexander implies that wartime brutality can cause unnecessary death and destruction through the Monkey's immoral behavior. In this case, it causes Stock's death:

> They rode into a clearing. The Monkey had already dismounted.
>
> Theo jumped down from his mare. What looked like a side of beef had been propped against a tree trunk. The eyes were open, staring at him. The mouth seemed full of red mud. It took him several minutes to realize it was Stock.
>
> Theo grew aware of the Monkey cursing endlessly and monotonously. He paid no attention. Something had to

be done about Stock's body; this seemed a matter of great importance. He stood for what he felt was a long time, considering what would be best. Rosana and the others in Stock's party lay awkwardly about the turf. Like the poet, they had been stripped and badly cut up. The Monkey was giving some kind of instructions about burying them. (*Kestrel,* 132–33)

Alexander ends the scene by having Justin and Theo agree never to take prisoners after this. Then he tells the reader that Theo "was not sane enough to realize he had gone somewhat mad; he had only gone mad enough to believe himself completely sane" (*Kestrel,* 134), and Theo becomes a tragic hero.

Throughout *The Kestrel,* Theo's moral conscience is ruled by uncontrolled passion. Because he feels that he failed in the last war, he determines to make amends for his lack of courage. He defies Florian's orders, sneaks out of Florian's headquarters, and becomes an aggressive and not always honorable leader within the guerrilla camp. His behavior resembles Justin's. In the end, Theo becomes Kestrel to his followers, and he acts as a bird of prey. Like the bird, he and his raiders utter bloodcurdling screams when they go into battle. They leave no survivors. His reputation as a fearless and bloodthirsty leader brings in new recruits. Alexander uses Theo to show the horrors of war, the way it drives people to become inhumane. Alexander's male protagonist is a sympathetic character, but he causes the reader to react uncomfortably to his changing personality. He cannot be the story's champion.

The real hero in this second book is Mickle. She assumes the typical questing pattern of the adventure story. She leaves the castle, saves the country and, indirectly, Theo from ruin, and returns to rule in a more democratic way. Her virtue never falters. Once outside the castle, she becomes the leader of her armed forces. She chooses a young soldier named Witz, a man who refused to abandon the monarchy and surrender to the invading army, to help her run the war. Witz is a mathematical genius who can predict the possible results of military action. He soon learns that his new monarch will not settle for military campaigns that involve large projected casualty rates. Each battle must be planned so that as few soldiers as possible will be lost. Thus, Mickle is intent upon saving lives while Theo is intent upon a bloody revenge.

Alexander develops a strong female character for his audience. He shows his reader that Mickle is in command of her troops in his scene of the first battle, and he confirms that she will be the favorite of the common soldiers:

> The queen, they decided, belonged first and foremost to them; no one else had quite the same right to claim her.
> "You should have seen it," said one of them. "A chit of a girl, jawing back and forth with us, cheeky as a bantam rooster. She's got a tongue in her head, too. Better than a mule driver."
> Another added, "Beggar Queen, some call her. Well, I say we could have used more beggars like her in the Col."
> (*Kestrel*, 49)

Established as the darling of the people, she need not reappear in the story until the climax of the action. The reader has seen that she is a first-rate leader, one loved and respected by her people.

Mickle has no figurative monkey on her back; the reader senses that she knows what is best for the country and that she will fend for herself. Throughout the book, Mickle is portrayed sympathetically. Her role as war leader and queen will merge by the end of the story when she rules both her troops and her kingdom, and she will become the story's true heroic figure. However, before Mickle finally returns to the story's action, Westmark is in grave danger.

Alexander reaffirms that Mickle is the hero of this book by having her devise a daring plan that will bring an honorable peace to the country. She proposes to escape behind the enemy lines disguised as a Regian officer, taking her loyal friend, the charlatan Las Bombas, with her. She plans to encounter King Constan-

tine and to negotiate peace. And so she has become the heart and
the brains of the story. In typical heroic tradition, she leaves the
safety of her followers and strikes out on her own. Once she is
placed on the road, Alexander has established a collision course
for the other major characters of the war.

Young King Constantine and Cabbarus have determined that
the country's immediate ruin is not a concern. They wish to rid
the kingdom of its beggar queen and to rule it on their own. In
contrast, Mickle has continually retreated whenever Constantine's Regians have drawn too close. Prior to leaving, Mickle assures Witz that her troops shall not fight. She prefers peace
brought through political negotiations to wartime victory.

Although Mickle is the hero of the adventure, she is not the
character whom the reader wants to follow. Theo has been developed as the more complex personality, and his fate is more interesting. Alexander realizes this and switches the story back. Once
again, Alexander emphasizes that Theo is less than heroic.

Alexander builds the final drama to its fullest and has the factions descend upon Eschbach, a small town surrounded by rough
terrain. As in *Westmark*, Alexander's main heroic characters descend upon a place chosen by the enemy only to win the battle
and restore the nation's order. Alexander carefully interweaves
his subplots within a series of quickly related events. Again, he
uses circumstances to resolve the conflicts.

Since Mickle is the questing hero, she must try to save the others. She tries to save Justin, but in the end fate intervenes and
the villagers choose that instant to revolt. The village episode
ends with a cliffhanger—Las Bombas tells Mickle, "Run for it! . . .
They think we're Regians!" (*Kestrel*, 194).

Immediately, Alexander switches his attention to Theo so that
his inner turmoil can be exposed. The reader watches Theo's anger build as he learns of Rina's death, faces Justin's fury for dis-
obeying Florian's orders, and discovers that Luther is dead. In a
rage he shoots at two fleeing Regians and hits Mickle. Then Alexander causes Theo to change: "His rage vanished, driven out by
a new horror of what he had done. Everything around him turned
into a nightmare. The stench of old blood caught in his throat. He

saw Stock's body again, and the Monkey, the kestrel's shrieking rang in his ears. All of it had brought him to this and had, finally, swept away even Mickle" (*Kestrel,* 200–201). Alexander has tied Theo's actions to his building anger and has shown how it turned him into a monster. When Las Bombas forgives Theo, he adds, "My dear boy, I hardly knew you. You looked like a madman. I could have taken you for—why, even for the bloodthirsty fellow, Kestrel," and Theo replies, "I am Kestrel. . . . No, I was Kestrel" (*Kestrel,* 203).

Theo's inner turmoil is calmed, but he is not healed. Alexander does not gloss over the effects of the war. Later, he will return to Theo as a tragic hero. For now, he can wind down the second book in his series.

With Justin out of physical danger and Theo diverted from his path of moral destruction, Alexander turns his story to Mickle's final chance encounter. Weasel and Sparrow, the water rats from *Westmark,* have been on the road, pursuing Keller. In the rough area surrounding Eschbach they encounter and capture a Regian officer who has fled the battle. Once overtaken, the officer, who turns out to be Constantine, agrees not to try to escape. Now that he has seen the horrors of war, he wonders out loud to his two captors, "Do you know—I used to play with toy soldiers" (*Kestrel,* 211). Two pages later the water rats come upon the wounded Mickle. Instantly, Theo and Las Bombas appear. Las Bombas recognizes Constantine, Mickle introduces herself, the negotiations begin, and the story comes to a conclusion.

However, Alexander adds a few twists to let the reader know there is more to come. First, the formerly charming Justin blames Theo for Rina's death and becomes Theo's personal antagonist. Second, Theo discovers that Montmollin was Florian's father. Thus, the ideal revolutionary is a young man who is waging war against a father's legacy. Third, Constantine reveals to Mickle that his uncle and his uncle's followers would be happier if he were out of the way, and we are left with Constantine's future in jeopardy. Finally, Theo cannot fully resolve his inner problems. At first, he retreats from the center of action to draw portraits of the men he knew in their moments of anguish, and this heals him enough to return to Mickle's side. He is still, however, at odds with himself.

Inside the court, Justin threatens rebellion, and, while Florian promises no immediate revolution, his remarks leave open the possibility. He is still uneasy about royal supremacy. He tells Mickle there will be no uprising, "not for the moment. What may come someday doesn't concern me now" (*Kestrel*, 242).

As the book ends, Mickle returns to an uneasy kingdom and places the monarchy in the guiding hands of three consuls, herself, Florian, and Theo. The battlefield has shifted from the war torn countryside to the chambers of the castle. Furthermore, Theo and Mickle have not reached a satisfactory conclusion to their relationship. Theo will serve the government, and as long as he is in this capacity he will not be allowed to marry the queen.

The Beggar Queen

The final book of the trilogy, *The Beggar Queen,* is divided into four rather than three parts, signaling a break with Alexander's mimicking of the classical apprenticeship novel. Within the final episodes Alexander will break ties with classical patterns. The story will not follow a typical bildungsroman path, and it will not contain a traditional happily-ever-after ending.

Alexander's dedication for *The Beggar Queen* reads, "For the old, who are children of their past. For the young, who are their own best hope for the future." In this book Alexander shows a shifting of old values to new ones, an exchange of old leaders for young ones, and a linking of the heroes' pasts to their futures. His actions reveal a sense of fatalism concerning political events combined with a belief in man's need to confront and struggle with his morality.

The main young protagonists for the first two books, Theo and Mickle, are adults now. They have assumed leadership roles, and they have reputations to live up to as they begin their final adventures in Westmark.

Theo will come into the future by letting go of the past; he must accept the fact that he caused Justin's injury and move on to help others. Yet at the book's beginning he cannot forget his first battle and continues to blame himself for Justin's disfigurement. Until Justin's death in the end, Theo is possessed with a desire to prove himself a fearless avenger for a just cause.

As the story begins, Theo has put his past as the bloodthirsty war leader Kestrel behind him. This time he and Mickle are living in the city. When Cabbarus storms Westmark and takes over the palace, the young heroes do not start out on a journey. They remain as outcasts hiding in the royal city and planning to overthrow the military government established by Cabbarus. Theo's actions are sanctioned by Mickle until he travels out of the city and faces Justin prior to the country's final uprising. Justin demands that Theo's people prove themselves by becoming involved in guerrilla activities, and Theo begins to consider this course of action. When Justin demands that Theo's townspeople act as guerrilla fighters, Mickle sees through Theo's dilemma and realizes that he will sacrifice others to prove his bravery. Alexander writes:

> "You'll give it. You. Are you trying to show him what your people can do? Or what you yourself can do? Is it Justin's good opinion of the Marianstat resistance? Or of you?"
> "It makes no difference what Justin thinks of me."
> "Are you sure?"
> "Of course I am."
> Mickle saw his face flush. She said no more, sensing it would only lead to a quarrel.
> It was the first time he had lied to her.[5]

Thus, Alexander emphasizes that Theo's past continues to haunt him, and he suggests that Theo's moral behavior suffers from his need to prove himself. After Justin is killed in one of the final skirmishes between the townsfolk and Cabbarus's soldiers, Theo recognizes what he has been doing and why he has been doing what he has done. Alexander tells his readers that Theo has been trying to prove himself to Justin and that he has still not come to terms with his past, commenting that "Justin had died, and he still was not free of him" (*Queen,* 197).

Theo's conflict between pacifism and war is carefully developed within the action. Thus, Theo has more than one moral problem that haunts him. He also continues to be faced with the results of his decision to banish Cabbarus from the kingdom rather than have him killed. Early in the action Justin says that Cabbarus should have been killed, and he adds, "He wasn't. We can thank the queen's lapdog for that. . . . He had the chance. What he didn't have was the stomach for it" (*Queen,* 19). Justin goads Theo into actions he would otherwise shun. His barbed remarks turn Theo into a man consumed once again with war. This time, Theo hopes to turn the past away, to make amends for his "cowardice" by single-handedly killing Cabbarus. Instead, he is caught and de-livered to Cabbarus.

Alexander has come full circle in his last book. Many of the events that happened at the end of the first book recur. This time they reach closure. The scene in which Theo is handed over to Cabbarus is a mirror picture of the one at the conclusion of *West-mark.* In *The Beggar Queen* Theo's fate is once again in the hands of Cabbarus. Theo realizes the truth: "As for Cabbarus, the man's life or death was a detail. The wheel would turn for Cabbarus, too. He would be destroyed: if not now, one day" (*Queen,* 208).

Theo represents Alexander's strong ties to existential thought. Theo has been free to make decisions that affected him and oth-ers, and he has had to accept responsibility for the results of his actions. Once he recognizes that his decisions have caused certain actions, but that the results of his decisions have gone beyond his control, he is free to reformulate his world. At the end of the series Theo is ready to rebuild himself.

Although Theo is Alexander's central intellectual hero, he is not the hero of the series. In the end, Mickle, who represents man's pragmatic nature, is a more heroic figure. Throughout the series Mickle places a high value on human life. Furthermore, she be-lieves in the future and in people's capacity to build a better world by correcting their mistakes with practical alternatives. Influ-enced by her past experiences, she is unwilling to accept the idea that she must always rule the country. Yet, she determines that she will supervise Westmark's affairs until a more proper solution is found.

Alexander has continually foreshadowed Mickle's rejection of the throne. In the first book she discusses who the ruler of Westmark should be, saying, "There must be a royal cousin somewhere who's foolish enough to like this kind of work," but then she concludes, "I'll stay here. For now, at any rate" (*Westmark*, 188–89). In *The Kestrel* she ends her journey with the comment that though she would like to give up ruling, "I don't trust anyone here not to botch it up—with all the best intentions. Not even Florian. Certainly not you, Justin. So, as for giving up the throne, I've decided: I won't" (*The Kestrel*, 241–42). In the final book, she reveals that she has discovered Florian's past, that she knows he is the cousin who could sit on the throne once she abdicates. Then she adds, "The people didn't give Marianstat to Florian or anyone else. . . . They took it. They took it for themselves. And all of Westmark, too. I've abdicated in their favor. The countryside belongs to them. They'll decide what to do with it" (*Queen*, 234).

Mickle explains that she decreed herself married to Theo long ago and agrees to be exiled from Westmark with him. They have come full swing in their adventures. In the final conversation between Theo and Mickle, Alexander reaffirms that Mickle is the true hero. She admits that she has regrets in losing her right to remain in the country, but shows her faith in the common citizens of Westmark when she says, "Are you afraid they'll make a mess of things? If they do, at least it will be their own mess. They'll straighten it out for themselves. Besides, there's always Sparrow. There's always Weasel. And others like them to help set things right" (*Queen*, 237).

Indirectly Sparrow and Mickle have been linked since *Westmark*. Alexander has continually likened Mickle to a street sparrow in his descriptions of her. He has named her the beggar queen, and Sparrow has been called a water rat. Both names bring to mind unsavory characters who make their ways by scavenging the spoils of others. In the last book, the linkage of the poor and the ruling classes is complete. During their adventures in *The Beggar Queen* the water rats become the "best hope for the future" alluded to in Alexander's dedication.

In *The Beggar Queen* Sparrow is not unlike the young Mickle of *Westmark*. Because she adores Keller, who is "Old Kasperl," the journalist who had earlier helped to inspire the general public to revolt, she has been "civilized" into wearing dresses. Under the able guidance of Keller and Theo, she has learned to read and set type. When Sparrow first appears in *The Beggar Queen,* she is sitting on the floor chatting with the princess in the journalist Keller's house. Alexander writes, "Their previous professions had been enough alike for them to form a fond sisterhood" (*Queen,* 25). Later, during the uprising, Sparrow re-creates Old Kasperl, writing the columns in a style similar to Keller's earlier ones and arranging to have the documents published by an unsuspecting member of the government's press.

Weasel becomes the war leader that Theo can never be. He also adores Keller, and he becomes the eyes and ears of a new generation in revolt. He causes Cabbarus's army a good deal of suffering when he builds a ramshackle barricade across one of the roads leading to the palace and brings a troop of street urchins together to form a military unit. As part of the hope for the future, these motley children are able to outwit the enemy on the doorsteps of the palace.

Sparrow and Weasel have had hard times; they have lived by foraging from the river and have seen war. Yet because neither one has been responsible for the physical or psychological destruction of a mentor or a friend, they have not been demoralized by the war. Sparrow comes closest, suffering personal anguish when she finds Keller near death. Alexander writes:

> Sparrow plunged past the officer and threw herself on Keller. His eyes were open, he was able to recognize her.
>
> "What have you done?" Sparrow burst out. "Keller, you're a fool."
>
> "So it would seem." He smiled at her. "My dear water rat—" He raised a hand to her cheek. "My dearest water rat."

> He was quiet. Bracken tried to draw her away. Sparrow gave an animal cry.
>
> "Keller! Keller, you can't do this." She clenched her fists as if she meant to pound life back into him. "I love you."
>
> It was the first time Sparrow had ever said that. (*Queen,* 168)

Sparrow is not responsible for Keller's death, and through his death she learns to express her love. And so, though the loss is great, it spurs her into acceptable wartime activities and forces her to voice her emotions. It does not destroy her psyche.

The news of Keller's death reaches Weasel when he is caught up in the fighting on the streets. Alexander writes, "Keller was dead, but it was Keller who saved him at last" (*Queen,* 181), and then he shows a determined Weasel who leads the others in the construction of the barricade. Weasel then becomes a street general in retaliation for Keller's death, and he fights for his mentor's ideals. Weasel's transformation from street waif to "Citizen Weasel" shows his building character. Unlike Justin and Theo, he has no dark memory to haunt him. His leadership will be more positive.

Both Sparrow and Weasel will be pragmatic leaders. Because they have been nurtured by Keller, they believe in truth and freedom of the press. Because they have had Theo and Mickle as friends, they will appreciate the need to listen to others. In the end, they can bring about a better government.

In 1982, when asked whether he was a realist or an optimist, Alexander explained that he was a "closet Romantic." He went on to say, "I'm a firm believer in Murphy's Law: If anything can go wrong, it will. I'm much aware that the bad guys usually win—but not always. I'm also much aware that the good guys never quit trying—and mustn't. I don't know if this is optimism. I'd say, rather, I'm not so much an optimist as a hopeful-ist."[6]

The country visited in the Westmark series is a war-torn one. Nothing has been solved in a magical way. Each battle has had its negative consequences. Not all have been ones that the heroes would have chosen. Furthermore, the odds seem stacked in favor of the villains. Eight major characters who sided with Theo and Mickle are dead; only four evil characters have died. The series is neither a fantasy nor romantic fiction. It is a turning point in Alexander's writing. Armed with historical and philosophical knowledge, the author has created a psychological novel that interprets the psychological life of its male protagonist and shows the dangers of living through our pasts.

The Westmark series is a remarkable addition to children's literature. It represents a new kind of writing, a cycle that depends upon history, philosophical ideals, and realism tempered with optimism. It suggests that modern fiction writing is not simplistic. It evades easy analysis, even when the story's plot reaches closure.

8

Elementary Stories

In 1981, Alexander discussed fantasy as a genre at the Simmons Symposium on Children's Literature. He remarked, "If the work contains an element of the impossible (at least as we currently understand the word), we classify it as a fantasy; if the work does not contain this element, if its events could indeed physically happen in the real world, we classify it as realism. I should add immediately that this is simply a categorical convenience. The difference is technical, not aesthetic."[1] Alexander had determined that there was a critical arbitrariness to genre categorizations. He was weary of being asked to talk to audiences as "an established author of children's fantasies." Like Frank Stockton, the earlier Philadelphian whose famous short story "The Lady or the Tiger" was used as a yardstick for all of his later works, Alexander's works seemed destined to be compared with the Prydain series, to be categorized as "yet another fantasy story."[2] The reviews of the Westmark series helped to dispel the illusion that he was only a fantasy writer, but they still pointed out stylistic and thematic similarities between this and his older series.

After finishing the Westmark series, Alexander was physically and emotionally drained. He had put many of his wartime experiences and memories into the series, and he needed to turn away from that part of his life. He needed to create a different kind of fiction, a fiction which could hold commentary about contemporary problems without seeming to hold any messages at all.

His intended audience had always been the youngsters who read his books for pure enjoyment. Although Alexander acknowledges that his intended audience is less experienced with the classics than he was as a youth, he has frequently mentioned various stories read during his childhood that have influenced his writing and has suggested similarities between his books and his childhood favorites. He has talked about his early enjoyment of Dickens's characterization, Tolstoy's realism in *War and Peace,* and the particular atmosphere of British Victorian fiction.

In 1971 he argued that all stories essentially ponder the same questions and all writers "draw from a common source."[3] When writing or talking about the elements of literature, he quoted Northrop Frye and Joseph Campbell, both noted for their archetypal criticism, and talked about stylistic similarities among various authors.

Alexander has reminded his critics that there is something elementary in all stories. He has suggested that authors do not create in a vacuum. They learn from the writings of those who established archetypes in literature and then redefine the plots, characters, and themes of the old stories to fulfill the needs of their contemporary audiences. For the inexperienced reader who has never read the earlier book, this new story is the archetype. It becomes a touchstone and frame of reference for future reading.

Once he had finished the Prydain series, Alexander began to concentrate his critical discussions on the author's responsibility to his audience and his need to contemporize his style. As early as 1969, he reasons in *Saturday Review,* "Every generation has to find its own tonality in art-style as well as in life-style. . . . The novel still seems, even today, the most adequate literary vehicle to express coherently, in breath and depth, basic human attitudes, emotions, and values."[4]

Throughout his discussions of writing, Alexander has maintained a conscious link between his writing and his childhood reading. That link is important in understanding the significance of the Vesper Holly series. As a child, Alexander read Dickens and

Arthur Conan Doyle. Both of these earlier writers created their literature serially, and both kept the average reader in mind as they wrote. Dickens first published his books as episodes in magazines, using cliff-hangers at the end of every episode. Alexander adopted that style from the beginning of his fictional career. Dickens created scenes that seemed lifelike by populating them with intriguing characters engaged in lively conversation. Alexander became a master at storytelling through conversation. Doyle used first-person narrative to win the confidence of his reader, a technique Alexander employed in the Vesper Holly series. Doyle told his stories from the point of view of the protagonist's companion, not the protagonist himself, so that the narrator could comment on the protagonist's abilities at sleuthing, and Alexander determined to have his Vesper stories told by the heroine's sidekick, a bumbling but endearing American professor.

Both Dickens and Doyle created a London scene that seemed real to their readers but that contained highly melodramatic incidents and characters. Both refused to write down to their readers. They assumed that the dramatic plot with its seemingly familiar background would be enticement enough for the general reader. Alexander wrote with the same premise. Although Doyle's Sherlock Holmes does not learn something about life by the end of the story, Dickens's heroes do. Alexander's new series involves heroes who learn about humanity and getting along with others by becoming involved with the ultimate sleuthing heroine in children's literature, Vesper Holly.

As a reader of Doyle, Alexander knew that mystery writers can write about their dreams without seeming to write "serious novels," and the creation of the Vesper series allowed him a forum for this. Unlike fantasy and realism, mystery is rarely taken seriously in the critical arena. Few books of criticism have been written on the genre, and those that have usually begin with an almost apologetic introduction about the author's choice of subject. As a result of this attitude, Doyle's popular books are seldom shared in today's high school English classes. When the mystery genre is introduced in most school literature programs, attention is instead given to the tales of Edgar Allan Poe. Few teachers recognize that while Poe established the conventions of the mystery story and is of archetypal significance, Doyle broke ground in narrative technique and tone. In creating the Vesper series, Alexander accepted a challenge similar to that faced earlier by Doyle: to write mysteries that would be critically recognized as noteworthy additions to the already existing "quality literature" for today's youths. Could he write in a genre that has rarely been taken seriously without ruining his reputation? Could he make a popular female sleuth who could appeal to the youthful audience used to reading about Nancy Drew and the Hardy boys without having the critics feel short changed?

Alexander had proven that he could write stories that would appeal to young readers, whether they were liked by the critics or not. Writing mysteries would allow him to pursue subversive ideas that young people would understand without having the adult critics pay much attention. In short, he could write antiestablishment stories that his youthful audience would appreciate without offending the older generation.

Critic Robert Newsom has discussed the author's need to depend upon his audience's background, and he has maintained that readers use multiple frameworks when deciphering fiction. They collect "evidence from the 'real' world and evidence from the 'fictional' world" to ascertain the probability of plot and characterization for the stories they read.[5] Alexander sought to combine the conventions of the detective/adventure story with the realities of proper behavior in the 1800s to produce a mystery that seemed plausible to his twentieth-century youthful readers.

Doyle and Alexander

There are many similarities between the Sherlock Holmes stories and the Vesper series. Some are conventions common to mystery stories. For example, it is not unusual to have two detectives working together to solve a mystery. Sherlock Holmes had Dr. Watson, Charley Chan had his son, and Nancy Drew never worked alone. Almost all literary detectives have existed outside of official law enforcement organizations; most are competing with the established arms of justice to solve the mystery first. Many stories have an ultimate villain who reappears in several adventures, for example, Doyle's Moriarty. Alexander used these conventions and elements specific to Doyle's work in his series.

Both Vesper and Holmes have distinctive physical appearances that set them apart from the rest of society. Holmes is tall and thin, smokes a pipe, and dresses in what has come to be identified as the appropriate "sleuthing costume." Alexander first describes Vesper in the third chapter of *The Illyrian Adventure* as "a girl of sixteen, almost my height, with sharp green eyes and waist-long hair of an astonishing marmalade hue. She wore a red caftan and purple slippers."[6] Because he has informed the reader in the previous paragraph that the year is 1872 and the setting is the Holly estate in Strafford, near Philadelphia, Vesper's appearance is striking. Young women had long hair in those days, but proper aristocratic young ladies wore their hair in carefully maintained coiffures, and nice girls did not wear flowing eastern garb. Both Holmes and Vesper have a restless air about them, which is soothed by playing music. Holmes plays Alexander's own instrument, the violin. Vesper plays a banjo, an instrument that would appeal to today's young readers.

Holmes and Vesper refuse to be daunted by conventions of society. In fact, they appear to flaunt their disdain for high society's stagnation. Holmes uses cocaine. Vesper dresses regularly in harem pants. Their Bohemian appearances and attitudes are obvious to their intended audience. Both are protagonists who live outside of genteel society and make their own rules. They are renegades who can solve society's mysteries without agreeing to become a part of that life.

As sleuths, they solve mysteries, but they don't retell them. Instead, their conventional sidekicks report their activities to the reader. Holmes is observed by Dr. Watson, a man of medicine who is well aware of Holmes's cocaine habit. Vesper's companion is the stodgy old Professor Brinton "Brinnie" Garrett who is well aware that Vesper doesn't quite fit into the eighteenth-century mode.

Alexander makes this clear in the first paragraph of the first book when he begins with Brinnie's observation that "Miss Vesper Holly has the digestive talents of a goat and the mind of a chess master. She is familiar with half a dozen languages and can swear fluently in all of them. She understands the use of a slide rule but prefers doing calculations in her head. She does not hesitate to risk life and limb—mine as well as her own. No doubt she has other qualities as yet undiscovered. I hope not" (*Illyrian,* 3).

Alexander's use of the first-person narrative appeals to readers who feel as if they are being given clues ahead of the detective. The conversational tone of the text suggests that the hero is worth discussing. The reader is not primarily focused upon finding the culprit but is intent on enjoying the cleverness of the protagonist's deductions. In the end, the reader learns not to trust the judgment of the reporter—he is less capable of discovering the answers to a mystery than the reader is. The narrator, instead of becoming a hero, can only create one in his reporting. His strength is his storytelling abilities.

Both Sherlock Holmes and Vesper Holly have talents that are never fully explained. Their earlier existence is never fully disclosed. In Vesper's case, Professor Garrett meets his new charge after she has been left to his guardianship by her father, the illustrious Dr. Benjamin Rittenhouse Holly. His death on the Greek island Mykonos is not explained. Although Vesper is always sympathetic to others and is highly educated, thanks, the reader assumes, to her father, she does not mourn his death.

Furthermore Vesper is a full-fledged orphan. Professor Garrett never mentions her mother. From the very beginning, the reader knows that Vesper is a wealthy and talented teen who is used to making decisions and having her own way. Her mysterious beginnings, like those of Holmes, are left to reader speculation.

Both Holmes and Vesper are mysterious characters who entice the reader into each new episode. The plot's outcome, like the hero's past, is never certain. And yet, it is. In the case of both sleuths, once the narrative establishes the characterization, the tempo, and the romanticized atmosphere, the reader anticipates that the detective will solve the crime. The predictability of plot and of detective are elements adroitly employed by Doyle and Alexander.

Alexander's stories can be appreciated at a different level by the reader who has read Doyle, but they need not have read Doyle. As mysteries, the Vesper stories create a world of their own. Alexander creates adventures that will entertain without depending upon the reader's understanding of the mystery genre.

When Alexander finished the Westmark series, he turned to Philadelphia for inspiration. He decided to depict the life of its wealthy elite, to use the Philadelphia area as the home site for his series. By setting his stories in the 1870s, Alexander was able to fulfill his urge to write about the city's upper-crust, intellectual community without appearing unrealistic. He could include the family names of prominent families such as the Rittenhouses.

The first four books begin and end in Philadelphia. The last adventure is set entirely in Philadelphia. Alexander says that he had to conclude the adventures there since the story was to take place in 1876, the year when America celebrated its centennial and Philadelphia hosted the Centennial Exposition. The reader senses that Alexander's narrator is showing his reader historic Philadelphia in a new light, making it seem realistic because it is based upon historical documentation, but creating a heightened scene that is melodramatic. In his "Author's Note" at the end of *The Philadelphia Adventure,* Alexander says that Vesper "adventures in a real place that seems imaginary, even fantastic: Philadelphia. Readers may well ask: How much is fact, how much is fiction?"

Each of the Vesper stories stands on its own. Each contains a new plot developed in a new setting. One story might refer to the happenings of another, but readers can read any adventure without reading the others. The character development is also not dependent upon past experiences. Similar themes and happenings, however, are found throughout the series. Their recurrence emphasizes Alexander's rationale for writing these adventures: helping youngsters define the moral implications of industrialism, commercial progress, and colonialism.

Alexander did a great deal of research before writing any one
of Vesper Holly's adventures. He wanted his stories to be set in
specific locales linked to historical happenings which seemed to
repeat themselves in other places and times and would, therefore,
seem to be current social concerns to his modern reader. In order
to find just the right link, Alexander read about the history of
countries facing humanitarian issues. He contemplated the landscape of a particular country and mapped out an imaginary world
that coincided with a real one. He studied the controversial cultural issues and embedded those in his plot. Thus, his adventures
contain a key to realism a link to the past that joins it to the
present.

His second book in the series contains the most historically rec-
ognizable plot. *The El Dorado Adventure* is partially based on
American filibuster expeditions into the Caribbean prior to the
Civil War. During the mid-1800s, American expansionists argued
that peoples of the Caribbean needed to be liberated from autocratic governments and archaic conditions. Using this logic as a
rationale for military invasion, a group of volunteer soldiers led
by William Walker put together an illegal military expedition and
sailed to Nicaragua. Walker had dreams of grandeur. He hoped
to gain dominance over all the countries of Central America. Although this filibuster became president of Nicaragua in a controlled election, he was forced out of the country after several
months of fighting. Walker did not give up. He reorganized and
returned again with some of his earlier followers and new recruits. In the end, Walker was executed by the Honduran
government.

Alexander researched the Nicaragua affair, but he did not limit
himself to pre–Civil War invasions. He looked at earlier and later
attempts to build canals and annex territories in all of Latin
America, including the attempts by the Grant administration to
annex the Dominican Republic during the Reconstruction years.
He understood the aims of the interlopers and the anger felt by
the local populace who resented foreign intrusion. He also knew
that today's youngsters were faced with new governmental intervention in Latin America and that they were concerned about

their country's support of the contras in Nicaragua. Alexander projected twentieth-century concerns onto eighteenth-century Latin America to show how foreign intervention inspires native insurrections and ultimately cripples economic stability and stifles cultural understanding. But the story was one that belonged to his two travelers.

Brinnie and Vesper

Alexander talked about travelers as narrators when he was at Simmons, saying that their tales "rank with fish stories and autobiographies, a few notches above political speeches." Then he went on to say that in fiction they become "flesh-and-blood characters like ourselves . . . [who] have been there ahead of us" and that "their messages are the most accurate we will ever get" ("Travel Notes," 60). If he created sympathetic characters who held his reader's attention, he could intersperse the adventures with philosophical and political statements. If his characters were overheard talking to one another, their conversations could not be considered didactic. They would simply be the conversations of "flesh-and-blood characters" who had seen insurrection and who gave us "the most accurate [messages] we will ever get." Within his plots, Alexander's characters discuss what intervention means, and they show how and why they react as they do.

The El Dorado Adventure begins when Vesper learns that her father won a large chunk of El Dorado in a poker game. She has been mysteriously summoned to discuss her claim with Alain de Rochefort. Despite Brinnie's protests, the two sail off to meet with de Rochefort. Prior to their meeting, however, Vesper meets Captain Blazer O'Hara, a man who fought with Simón Bolívar's revolutionary forces. O'Hara explains that de Rochefort wants to build a canal across the country. He goes on to say, "The Chiricas are smack in his way. But that's none of his worry. He'll turn their land into a lake bed, and themselves at the bottom of it, village and all. . . . The villain's clever as they come. If anyone can pull it off, he's the one to do it."[8] Furthermore, O'Hara points out that the government will get pay-backs from the toll that ships will have to pay when using the canal, and so it is supporting de Rochefort and ignoring the pleas of the natives to leave the river alone. Thus, Alexander has set up an adventure through conversation.

Once Vesper meets de Rochefort and asks him what concerns he has about taking over the land of the Chiricas, de Rochefort assures her that there is only a "small, scattered handful of the most backward savages, ignorant and superstitious" (El Dorado, 33) living in the area. He denies that his venture will have any effect on the land he has invaded. Alexander has established him as a typical entrepreneur.

When Vesper and Brinnie venture into the wilds, they meet the Chiricas's chieftain and make certain assumptions about his education based on misinformation about the native conditions. The chief Acharro chastises them for their assumptions. Vesper enters his home, and finds Euclid's geometry and a set of Rousseau. She discovers that the chieftain is an educated man and is impressed by his learning and his intellect. However, she soon discovers that the women in the village are not allowed to speak at the council meetings and that they do all of the work while the men engage in sports and council meetings. Our heroine is outraged at the village men's backwardness, but then she reminds the reader that the United States was equally backward in the 1800s, saying that women have no voice in the government of the United States and that if they try to change things, "our men lock them up in a jail, poke a tube down their throats and pour food into them if they won't eat" (El Dorado, 69). Thus, Alexander links past attitudes to present ones.

Vesper's relationship with Acharro subtly reinforces Alexander's message of imperialism. Although Vesper hopes to help the Chiricas keep their land for themselves, she does not wish to leave them without native industry. She seeks an economic answer to their problem. When she and Acharro travel to the notorious volcano, she discovers possible oil deposits, and she asks Acharro if he understands their value. Acharro retorts that he has no interest in ruining the land as Philadelphia was by Drake, and he concludes, "That would destroy us as much as the canal—in a different fashion, but just as surely" (*El Dorado,* 91). Vesper is forced to realize that the Chiricas will not "modernize" their lifestyle or change their land.

Later, the native women save the lives of Vesper, Brinnie, and Acharro, and Vesper demands that they be allowed to have a place in the village council. Once allowed to attend, Vesper suggests that the villagers can save themselves from economic ruin if they all work together to make the handicrafts that have previously been made by the women and argues that the work will not be "women's work" if the villagers all work at it. Alexander tells his reader, "There was, at first, a certain amount of indignation among the Caymans and Jaguars. In the end, however, the women carried the day" (*El Dorado,* 159). Thus, Alexander's heroine brings equality of the sexes into the jungle of El Dorado long before it comes to the United States. And, Alexander weds progress to native industry by having a reformed de Rochefort stay behind and put his engineering talents to use in helping the Chiricas develop more advanced looms and pottery wheels.

It is Alexander's carefully constructed first person narrative that adds character to the stories while helping the reader learn that events and people are not always what they seem to be on first evaluation. Alexander has Professor Garrett tell the story in a ironic, conversational manner. Garrett is a scholar who considers himself to be a man of the world. Brinnie recounts his first evaluations of the people and events, foreshadowing his lack of understanding and inability to make objective evaluations.

Professor Garrett is an ironic narrator who recounts his misjudgments in his retellings. He always values those who resemble himself. He looks upon "natives" with suspicion, and he prejudges events based on his limited experiences in Philadelphia's learned society. Since he had earlier traveled with Vesper's father and since his judgment does not improve much throughout the series, the reader senses that no amount of travel or adventure will make him truly objective. He is a class snob, though he is essentially a harmless one. He does learn to like those natives he meets individually, and he does change his attitudes about particular groups after following Vesper into battle. But he cannot tell a villain from a hero.

When, for instance, he first meets Dr. Desmond Helvitius in *The Illyrian Adventure,* Brinnie describes him as "garbed in heavy tweed knickers and a shooting jacket, he was a large, looming sort, who looked as if he spent more time outdoors than poring over manuscripts. His great shock of white hair added an air of benevolence and good nature" (*Illyrian,* 28). Brinnie remembers that Helvitius spoke with "the faintest shadow of an accent I could not identify" (*Illyrian,* 29), a clue to the reader that Helvitius is not all he seems. Thus, the reader is forewarned that Helvitius is hiding something and will not be surprised when Vesper points out that Helvitius doesn't seem to be telling the truth about his research concerning the Illyrian legend. However, because Helvitius outwardly appears to be a gentleman, Brinnie argues that Helvitius would not lie to them. On the other hand, Brinnie does not trust the local rebels, and so when Vesper hires a native Illyrian to be their guide, Brinnie describes him as "a gangling, large-framed fellow, his over-sized feet encased in scuffed leather boots, one of those Illyrian pill-box caps on the back of his head, his hair tumbling into his eyes. His gait was something between a slouch and a sulk" (*Illyrian,* 32). In the end, their guide turns out to be the rebel leader and the impersonator of the famous legendary Illyrian hero, Vartan.

Throughout the series, Brinnie remains incapable of evaluating people or events beyond surface levels. He argues for the establishment without sensing that his attitudes will keep the rich wealthy, the poor in dire straits. Yet, he accepts Vesper's judgment by the end of each adventure, and he records her questioning of the status quo with pride.

During the final story, *The Philadelphia Adventure,* Brinnie and Vesper become involved in political intrigue. Since the events take place in and around their native Philadelphia, Brinnie's narrative concerns his perceptions of American people and places. In this story, Alexander intersperses real personalities with imaginary ones to show how people shape events.

President Ulysses Grant comes to Vesper because the series'

ultimate villain, Helvitius, has named her as the person to act as
messenger in his latest scheme. Once again, Brinnie fails to see
things as they are. Brinnie recalls that Grant looked terrible on
their first meeting, saying, "His beard was a little scruffy, his face
tight-set, his complexion pallid. Never had I seen a man so bru-
tally burdened by the cares of high office. . . . Even his starched
collar appeared to be throttling him. No doubt he would have
been more happily at ease in the unbuttoned army jacket and
baggy trousers that Mr. Mathew Brady had immortalized in
photographs."

Brinnie remembers Grant as a wartime hero and excuses all of
the scandal in Grant's presidency. He never criticizes his leadership abilities, but simply states that the political scams surrounding Grant's administration have come "through no fault of his
own" (6).

Throughout, Brinnie insists on seeing American people in a
positive light. He accepts the argument that Grant's government
must stay intact if the United States is to survive. In a sense,
Brinnie is romanticizing Grant so that he can continue to believe
that the United States is a moral country.

Alexander uses fiction to emphasize Brinnie's need to believe
in the natural goodness of the common people. When he discovers
that the dock workers have agreed to help kidnap Vesper and
himself, he says, "To think that Philadelphians were open to this
wholesale bribery—it pained me" (43). Later, he first describes
General Gallaway as a dapper ex-soldier whose "jaunty dis-
array . . . must have taken careful study to achieve" (74). And,
though he listens to Gallaway's tirade against Grant's leadership,
he continues to trust Gallaway. When forced to admit that Gallaway is a scoundrel, Brinnie explains, "General Gallaway, at
present, might be something of a madman, but there was no de-
nying his past heroism; and certainly, a ranking officer of our
Grand Army of the Republic would never conspire with an arch-
fiend like Helvitius. I grasped at any straw to explain the unex-
plainable" (81).

To the youthful reader, Brinnie personifies well-meaning
adults who evaluate people and events in light of their cultural

upbringing. He never doubts the valor and honor of wartime heroes. And, he places a great deal of stock in appearances. The reader understands that Brinnie will never completely change his values, but that his attitudes will be softened by his exposure to Vesper, a person so unlike him in outward manners that he would not have chosen to oversee her activities had he not been obliged to "raise her." The very irony of his own narrative appeals to the contemporary teen; Brinnie is too old to see things straight, but he is not too old to be proud of the actions of the next generation. Brinnie makes the youthful reader feel smug about his own ability to judge events and situations with candor.

Vesper indirectly represents what Alexander wishes for the next generation. Her attitudes and relationships with others are freewheeling. Unafraid to dress differently, always vocally and physically fighting for the rights of the underdog, Vesper dares to risk her well-being for others. In the first four books she travels abroad. As an outsider who has little to gain from the country's struggles, she singlehandedly fights imperialism. And she teaches the warring peoples to listen to one another and to work towards tolerance and equality.

Vesper is always depicted as a strong heroine. As she leaves each foreign country she takes the gratitude of the natives with her, and she wins the affection of an admiring male who would sacrifice his life for her. The rebel leader in *The Illyrian Adventure* tells her, "You have done more than Vartan himself. Think of him as he thinks of you" (*Illyrian,* 131). The chieftain Acharro tells her, "There is none other in this world like Miss Vesper Holly" (161). The noble Tawarik leader An-Jalil says, "Should you lose your life, it will be only if I lose mine" (*The Jedera Adventure,* 80).

Vesper remains headstrong and independent throughout the series. She is never overshadowed by the native protagonist, and she is not prone to romantic fantasies. Even in *The Philadelphia Adventure,* when the love interest between Vesper and the young male protagonist is the strongest, Vesper is not caught in the web of matrimony. She is pulled from the Schuylkill River by the gawky Tobias Wistar Passavant, and it appears that she is smitten by this footloose Philadelphian. However, she seems unaware that Toby has saved her from mortal danger. Later, she explains that while in the river she struggled with Helvitius and picked his pocket, thus saving the visiting Brazilian ruler from political embarrassment. In the end, Toby, Vesper, and Brinnie's wife, Mary, conspire to take the four of them off on a new foreign tour. Vesper remains an adventurer.

Vesper is an intelligent heroine who enjoys intellectual challenges. Although she becomes involved in outrageous undertakings, her overseas trips begin in a scholarly fashion as she discovers something from the past. Her curiosity and desire to travel abroad are usually linked to reading and learning. In *The Illyrian Adventure,* which is fictiously linked to the classic epic *the Iliad,* Vesper is depicted as an inquisitive, knowledgeable young woman of sixteen who wants to solve a mystery left half discovered by her father. She approaches her trusty guardian, and explains, "He was onto something. He didn't say exactly what, but it convinced him he'd been right all along" (*Illyrian,* 8). Shortly afterward, she simply says, "I'm going to Illyria. And, Brinnie, so are you" (Illyrian, 9).

She is aware of the villains and their schemes before the narrator is. In *The El Dorado Adventure* Vesper decides to travel to Latin America once she is informed that her father has left her land in the country. Astute at traveling, once embarked she informs Brinnie that the trip could hold surprises. Alexander writes,

> "It never struck you, Brinnie? One-way tickets?"
> Vesper yawned and settled into her chair for an untroubled nap.
> I could not do the same. (*El Dorado,* 9)

She cajoles the professor into his adventures, usually with the help of his wife, Mary. Thus, Mary agrees that Brinnie needs a sea voyage in *The El Dorado Adventure,* is talked into attending the diamond jubilee celebration of the grand duchess in *The Drackenberg Adventure,* and maintains that Brinnie must return a library book once he has given his word in *The Jedera Adventure*. Mary's role as supportive ally is finally confirmed at the end of *The Philadelphia Adventure* when Brinnie observes, "During the days that followed, I saw little of The Weed; or for that matter, of Vesper and Mary. I was, however, aware that they were engaged in long conversations among themselves. Had I been of a suspicious turn of mind, I might have supposed they were up to something" (144). Throughout the stories, Brinnie's maintains his evaluation of Mary as a "dear soul" who is always sensible, practical-minded, and fair in her evaluations of others. Yet, by the end of the series the reader can see that Mary is not as delicate an angel as Brinnie imagines. Twice she escapes kidnapping attempts, and in the final episode she captures Gallaway's villainous henchman. Since she is left alone for long stretches of time, the reader perceives that she is used to being independent.

Though Vesper always tricks Brinnie into arranging her overseas trips, Brinnie does not consider her deceitful. He calls her a "dear girl" throughout their adventures, and he relishes the idea that he somehow is protecting her from undue danger by going along with her. Alexander's heroine, then, is capable of winning the admiration and trust of men, even when she outsmarts them.

Alexander has created a heroine who is a prototype for modern women to emulate. She is striking in appearance but not caught up in fashion, well read, capable of taking care of herself, interested in current affairs, sympathetic toward minorities, and sensible about her attachments.

Furthermore, Vesper is assumed to be the only one who can outwit the villain Helvitius. She is the ultimate heroine. Aware of scientific, historic, and artistic accomplishments, she matches wits with Helvitius, often beating him in the game of delusion. In *The Drackenberg Adventure,* when Helvitius shows Vesper the valuable Leonardo da Vinci painting he has obtained, Vesper implies that it is not as old as he thinks, suggesting that the paint used has nineteenth-century synthetic coloring and asking him, "Did you only see what you wanted to see? When you have time, after you get rid of us, take another look."[10] Never openly dishonest, Vesper later explains to Brinnie that she is sure that the painting is authentic and adds, "I didn't lie to him. . . . Not exactly. I only asked a few questions. He did the rest by himself" (*Drackenberg*, 121).

Alexander uses Vesper to show the importance of knowledge when battling against wrongdoers, but through Helvitius he reminds his readers that crooks also know much. The moral differences between these two pinpoint the difference between the actions of people who gain knowledge in order to help others and those who secure knowledge in order to control and manipulate others. Helvitius acknowledges that his plans call for the death and destruction of others. He admits that his admiration for Vesper's intelligence keeps him from killing her, but he never rules out that as a possibility. Vesper will not destroy anyone, but she would like to put Helvitius in jail. However, much as she would like to have him captured and punished, Helvitius is never caught. Thus, Vesper's and Brinnie's struggles for justice over corruption are never completed, and the reader is left with the reality that at times crime does pay.

The first four books fit a set pattern and all contain implied messages about foreign entrepreneurism. The last book breaks with the earlier ones in several ways, signifying that it is either the last in the series or the first of a series with the narrator and protagonist in a new relationship. Indirectly, it signals the end of the sleuthing duo. Brinnie first tells the reader, "Miss Vesper Holly welcomes visitors, even uninvited ones. . . . In some ways, I am sorry that she did" (3). The visitor he is directly discussing is the president, Ulysses Grant. However, he is also alluding to another unwelcome visitor who has changed his relationship with Vesper. In the third chapter the most unwelcome guest enters the scene. He is "The Weed." Brinnie says, "Tobias Wistar Passavant—Vesper had nicknamed him 'The Weed'—had arrived several months ago, unannounced and uninvited. He had returned from some sort of archeological expedition on the island of Crete. . . . Aware of Dr. Holly's own research, he begged Vesper to allow him to use her father's library. Vesper generously gave permission. This lanky, gawky individual had been in residence ever since" (16).

Toby is four years older than Vesper and is an attractive counterpart for the heroine. Like Vesper, his background is never fully explained. Like Vesper, he is accustomed to traipsing about the world, intermingling with the natives of the countries he visits, and solving mysteries. Like Vesper, he has unorthodox habits and is full of book knowledge.

To the reader, Toby is a hero. To Brinnie, he is a threat. The Weed is respectful of the professor. He calls him "sir" and assumes they share the same zeal for history and poetry. Brinnie complains that The Weed is too large in all ways, that "he is a one-man crowd" (16). His cheerfulness and playfulness bother Brinnie, partly because they appeal to Vesper. Brinnie continually complains about Toby's personality. Yet, he acknowledges that he appeals to Vesper.

Within this last book Vesper develops typical "daughterly" ways of flattering "dear old Brinnie." She gets Toby out of the way and flatters Brinnie into believing that she needs him near her. She sends Toby off to act as a decoy for the search party, and she has him stay behind to guard the children while she and Brinnie save the president and the Brazilian emperor.

However, Brinnie observes her respect for The Weed, and he senses that this is different from her earlier encounters with male counterparts. Throughout the adventure, he unconsciously begins to compare Toby to the others and discovers that Toby has a way with animals that is every bit as successful as the gypsy king in Drackenberg, that he has a reckless daring equaled only by the Illyrian rebel Vartan, that he is as good a tracker as Acharro of El Dorado. When, at last, Brinnie awakens to discover that he has been saved from drowning by The Weed, he admits to feeling "kindly disposed toward him" (139). Alexander is showing his reader that fathers suffer a good deal of regret when their daughters finally find someone who is their contemporary counterpart.

In the end, Vesper announces that she will travel to Crete with Toby, and Brinnie recalls his reaction: "I was too stunned to speak. Vesper leaving us? What thoughts crowded my mind in that instant: the dear girl's sun-blistered face during our crossing of the Haggar; her carefree laughter as we waltzed at Duchess Mitzi's diamond jubilee; our galloping through the Illyrian backlands; swimming the Culebra. And, with all that, my memory of

La Pierre House, Vesper in her red caftan, my terrible fear that I was seeing her for the last time, I had been correct, though in a way I had never imagined" (144). Though Brinnie and Mary will travel with Vesper and Toby, Brinnie will have a different role. He will be in the background of Vesper's life. The ending of *The Philadelphia Adventure* marks the beginning of Brinnie's realization that Vesper dreams of a new way of life, not too unlike the one they shared in their earlier escapades, but with Toby at her side instead of Brinnie.

Autobiographical Memories

Alexander's own daughter Madeleine shared many of his adult adventures with him. When he was stationed in Paris, they became fast friends, much like Brinnie and Vesper. Once in America, Madeleine rapidly adapted to a new culture and a new language. As an adult, she married a man from Lebanon. His wife Janine has much in common with Mary. She is supportive and intelligent. Her evaluations of events and people often ring true. She is loyal to Lloyd—and to Madeleine. Once in a discussion, Alexander said, "There is no such thing as a docile woman. All of the women whom I've met have been strong personalities, people who are involved with things." This series embodies that belief. It is a series written specifically for today's young female reader. Lloyd Alexander dedicated *The Illyrian Adventure* to his daughter and his grandchildren, and the next two books were dedicated to the "other Vespers" he had met.

The Vesper series has strength in its use of traditional characterization and structural patterns of the mystery genre. However, because Vesper is more alive and keen than many of her earlier literary prototypes, she can become the contemporary female reader's ideal sleuth. Vesper fits in today's literary world. Her adventures might surpass earlier reader response interpretations of the mystery novel in children's literature if youngsters are allowed to compare this series to the earlier standards set by Sherlock Holmes and Nancy Drew.

9

Critical Audiences

Lloyd Alexander has won the hearts of children and young teens who want hero stories with a good deal of adventure and mystery. His first youthful readers have read his books as they were published, eagerly following his literary career. When the Prydain series was first published, I was the bookmobile librarian for Madison Public Library in Madison, Wisconsin. One of my regular readers was a youngster about ten years old. He found *The Book of Three* on his own, and when he returned it, he asked for the sequel. I could hand him two more books, but then I had to tell him that the rest hadn't been written. Every week he would enter the bookmobile and ask for the new adventure. Most of the time, when I said that the next adventure wasn't out yet, he reread one of the first three.

Alexander talks about adolescents who began corresponding with him over twenty years ago. Some have made him models of characters from his books; a few have visited him at his home. They have become personal friends with shared interests. Because he has written sequels, they ask when he will write sequels to the single-volume stories he has produced.

Alexander once told me, "Some of my stories don't need a sequel, though I know I could write one that would sell." Alexander does not repeat what he does unless he feels a need to complete a cycle. And, when he writes a cycle he has a philosophical reason for the continuation. Because he is aware that his youthful readers have come to expect extended stories from him, he has used this format to create three successful series. However, he does not write second stories because they are marketable.

His Westmark books have an older group of readers than the Prydain books. These readers, too, correspond with Alexander. He has noticed that the fears and concerns of these twentieth-century teenage readers are different from those of the earlier Prydain readers. Recently he said, "It is surprising how many write about suicide and look at the Westmark books as ones which relate to their concerns."

The paperback editions of the Vesper series have followed on the heels of the Dutton hardback copies. By now both Dell and Dutton know that Alexander will sell. And they realize that there are two audiences for Alexander—the children's librarians who buy hardback editions and the youthful readers who can best afford to buy paperbacks.

Although the Disney movie based on the Prydain series was not a favorite with movie reviewers or with Alexander, it did introduce another youthful audience to Alexander's writing. The movie audience was more accustomed to seeing literature on the screen than reading it, but many turned to the books after seeing the movie. Accustomed to seeing and reading stories of high adventure, this newly formed audience is one that can appreciate Alexander's more recent mysteries.

The various awards Alexander has won throughout the years attest to his popularity among children's librarians and teachers. Although the top American awards were largely given to Alexander for his early fantasy writing, his Westmark series has received high recognition in Sweden, and his overall achievements have been acknowledged by the Catholic Library Association, the Church and Synogogue Library Association, and both the school and public library associations of Pennsylvania. Aware of readers and their interests, these groups have confirmed that Alexander is a popular writer who creates quality fiction.

Critical Evaluation

Yet, the world of academic scholars has failed to acknowledge Alexander's writing for its diversity or depth. Critics have been uninterested in exploring his continual shift in style and have not commented upon his redirection of his writing toward an older audience and away from the preteens who read his first series. Winner of the prestigious Newbery Award, Alexander has been acknowledged for his early fantasy series.

Early critical discussion of Alexander concentrated on his uses of Celtic legend in the Prydain books. Critics labeled Alexander a writer of "high fantasy" or of "sword and sorcery fantasy," creating stories that depend upon the adult Arthurian legends. Since Alexander has always admitted that Prydain is based on Celtic legend, the critics judged Alexander's success based on his adapting the adult materials found in *The Mabinogion* for youthful audiences. While scholars involved with high fantasy admit that Alexander's series was the first children's books in the twentieth century to successfully use *The Mabinogion* as its source for scenes and characters, many argue that he somehow fails. Some feel that Alexander's treatment does not accurately reflect the British Arthurian tales.

British critics, when they discuss Alexander, are especially critical. John Rowe Townsend is probably the best example of British reaction to Alexander. In an essay that discusses Alexander, LeGuin, Cooper, and Wrightson, Townsend calls Alexander "the most straightforward" of the children's fantasy authors and points out that Alexander does use real elements of *The Mabinogion.* However, he seems displeased, with Alexander's characterization. He concedes that the hero and heroine are Alexander's inventions, but he suggests that they are not right for the adventure. Taran and the other main characters, he says, are "two-dimensional", "predictable and in the end a little tiresome."[1]

C. W. Sullivan III, an American children's literature scholar who has written extensively about Celtic-based fantasies, has provided the most thorough discussion about Alexander's adaptation of the Celtic legend. Sullivan insists that Alexander's inspiration is the *Mabinogi* tales, but he points out that Alexander does not use the elements with consistency in his cycle, that he may use something only once, and that the main characters "are essentially of the author's own devising."[2] Sullivan separates his study of high fantasy from the work of Jack Zipes and Bruno Bettelheim, stating that he is interested in "how a mythology functions and what a fantasy author is trying to elicit from the reader" (*Sullivan,* xi). Sullivan's lucid commentary shows how Alexander incorporated elements from the Celtic original materials in order to create a new world of sorcery whose inhabitants evolve from myth.

Sullivan sees some changes within Alexander's finely drawn world that allude to the realities of Celtic history. Thus, Sullivan perceives Taran's acceptance of the position as High King and Eilonwy's loss of her magical powers when she becomes his queen as indicative of the change from one age of Celtic rule to another (*Sullivan,* 62–63). To Sullivan, the critics fail in their discussions of Celtic-based fantasy because they do not acknowledge the traditional strains as a "reference within which the author can construct the original material necessary to make the novel more than just a retelling of a traditional Celtic story" (Sullivan, 143–45).

In fact, critics seem to argue among themselves about Alexander's interpretation of the Mabinogi. While most suggest that his characters are unique but the details are accurate, some suggest that even the details are not quite right. Others have maintained that Alexander did not recreate the land of Wales, that his setting is his own invention based on his brief time in Wales. After living in Anglesey, Barbara Z. Keifer wrote, "While the Prydain chronicles are no doubt good books, their goodness does not come from a deeply felt sense of a *real* place but from motifs and characters borrowed from the ancient legends and from other elements of story such as characterization and plot."[3]

Laura Ingram's essay on Alexander discusses the problem of his setting and, indirectly, pinpoints, the central problem for critics who evaluate Alexander's series as an extension of the Welsh legend. Ingram acknowledges that, when compared to Tolkien, Alexander's landscape is less detailed, a plus, she says, for the young reader. However, she points out that those who study the Arthurian tales have viewed the series as being too contemporary, not dependent enough upon the ancient legends.[4] Indirectly she is suggesting that the Arthurian scholar is looking for a different sort of book than the real reader is.

The Arthurian critic wants to discuss the book's retelling of the Celtic legend and will judge the series a failure if it is too original. The young reader wants a book that reflects his concerns. Thus, archetypal criticism of Alexander pinpoints a problem in all archetypal criticism of contemporary children's fantasy stories: that criticism fails to acknowledge the author's perception of his intended audience.

Jack Zipes has argued that archetypal criticism that ignores the author's intent will ultimately fail. He suggests that fantasy is antigeneric because it is at odds with the conventions of society. He comments, "Each fantasy sets out to contravene not only the laws of nature and the conventions of society and aesthetics, but also seeks to establish itself as unique, to conceive a totally new world which has its own laws and values."[5] Critics of fantasy, Zipes suggests, must consider how the author extends his world's reality in the newly formed world. The emphasis should be upon the new elements in the story, not on the traditional trappings.

Such an argument calls for biographical criticism as the groundwork for analysis. Contemporary critics who wish to explore the works of Alexander can turn to the work of Michael O. Tunnell and James S. Jacobs for biographical information. Jacobs's "A Personal Look at Lloyd Alexander" contains a good deal of information that will give the critic insights into Alexander's style and his rationale for writing.[6] Jacobs argues that Alexander's texts cannot be judged unless the critic recognizes the link between his view of the world and his stories. He maintains Alexander's environment helps to determine his characterization and genre. Jacobs writes about Alexander's daily routine, attitudes, and past experiences. He does not analyze Alexander's writing, but concentrates upon making obvious connections between Alexander's themes and the contemporary attitudes of his country. Those who study Alexander should refer to Jacobs's work. Often this is not the case.

Critical opinion on Alexander's work has changed as new fields began to make an impact upon children's literature and as society's attitudes changed. Seldom is Alexander's past considered. The evolving criticism on the Prydain series shows the shift in interpretation.

Reviewers writing about the Prydain books in the sixties labeled Eilonwy a success. She was considered a liberated character set in the pattern of traditional fantasy. However, Alexander's interpretation of male and female roles came under attack in 1985 when Lois Kuznets, a professed feminist critic, wrote that Taran is not an example of the American ideal since he becomes High King, not president of his country, and since the female heroine never achieves womanhood in Alexander's story. Kuznets questions Alexander's intended message, adding, "Are these stories finally too intractable? Does the medium alter the message?"[7] Zipes, a Marxist scholar with sympathies toward feminist criticism, calls Kuznet's article "exemplary for the manner in which she deals with the characters, themes, and patterns of fantasy in regard to a traditional genre and contemporary issues" (Zipes, 190). Yet, Kuznets's interpretation suggests one of the major loopholes in some of the feminist criticism that has evolved in reaction to children's literature during the 1980s: it lacks sensitivity to Alexander's milieu. Alexander was writing the Prydain series in the mid-sixties, not in the 1980s, and his audience was just awakening to the positive attitudes of feminism. Early leaders of the movement were held in disrespect, and popular attitudes on women in society were only beginning to support new roles for women. Alexander's interpretation of a strong heroine is in step with his experiences. He had known strong women, from his mother to Gertrude Stein to his wife Janine. He expected them to speak out for those things they believed in, but he also watched them conform within the demands of society or accept ostracism. His princess becomes a queen because she chooses to accept the more traditional role of wife and supporter. Alexander's depiction of Eilonwy, however, suggests that she is a person with strong opinions and a sharp tongue, and his ending does not imply that she will mellow. Alexander's princess is not a feminist model, but a flesh-and-blood girl whose heritage is partly Celtic, partly contemporary. If Kuznet's arguments are to be considered exemplary by Zipes's own standards, she must take into account why the author wrote as he did; she cannot simply place her late twentieth-century attitudes upon the materials. Thus, critics who turn to Alexander as a source for feminist interpretation will fail unless they acknowledge that literature cannot be discussed without taking into account the author's society and other current literary movements. Fantasy criticism demands a more eclectic approach than it is normally given.

Critics have acknowledged that Alexander led the way in children's literature for future fantasy series writers when he wrote the Prydain series. He broke with the tradition of simply retelling the British Arthurian story by modernizing it for children so that they could see the story as true to their everyday experiences.

The series was selected by the Children's Literature Association as a "Touchstones Book" to be used as a yardstick when evaluating others. Jon C. Stott's *Touchstones* article on Prydain discusses the cycle as a male bildungsroman adventure and identifies its greatness in its major message "that each of us must face beginnings, must grow by entering brave new worlds."[8] Both the Children's Literature Association and the American Library Association have recognized that Alexander created something unique, that this series would last. Both referred to it as quality writing that could be appreciated by future youngsters. And, both commended Alexander for daring to try something not usually done in children's literature.

Once Alexander determined that he wished to try something else, to initiate another break from traditional children's stories, the university critics turned their backs on him and ignored his writing.

Laura Ingram has discussed the Westmark series, calling it "troubling" because it "proposes a paradox in exploring the confusing demands often made upon the human conscience in times of political upheaval" (Ingram, 52). Ingram's comment addresses the greatness of the series. The books deal with the psyche of man and the relationship between society's demands for heroism and humanity's needs for compassion. Alexander's descriptions of battle within the Prydain series are brutal, but they are not ones apt to have happened. In Westmark the events are more realistic and stark. His careful development of a political novel that depicts a war-torn country and the possibilities of corruption in times of upheaval makes this series unique in young adult literature.

When an author dares to defy traditions and break with established patterns in children's literature, is he going beyond the limits of typical archetypal interpretation? Can children's texts be deconstructed? Can authors show children that society's interpretations of heroism often contradict individual needs for self-determination?

Although critical opinion has not evolved for the Westmark series, a sense of its place in literature is emerging. *Westmark* was selected for the American Book Award in children's literature, signifying its recognition as an important contribution to the field. Upon its publication, *The Beggar Queen* was selected by the American Library Association as one of the best books for young adults, emphasizing that the series was apt to be popular with an audience different from the Prydain series readership, and attesting to its literary quality in the field of high school literature.

The Vesper series has been largely ignored also, but it is not without accolades. *The Illyrian Adventure* was an American Library Association Notable Book and won the Parents' Choice Award, showing, once again, that the adults who would share books with young people recognize Alexander as a man who writes quality literature for youngsters. Yet, the series has not been received as an innovative break with traditional patterns. The *New York Times Book Review* called the book predictable and stale.[9]

The lack of critical discussion may have to do with Alexander's choice of styles. Little criticism has been written on the children's mystery adventure story since Alexander began the Vesper books. An article by Carol Billman does suggest how Vesper fits into the field. Billman pointed out that there were few "tightly constructed whodunit a la Agatha Christie" children's mysteries when she was writing. Using the arguments of literary critic John Cawalti and of psychoanalyst Lilli Peller, she suggests that adolescents are continually striving to solve the secrets adults are hiding from them. She suggests that sleuthing is an enjoyable pastime for them. She argues that mysteries force young people to become participants in the reading process and that as they read conventional mysteries they learn how to "match wits with the author."[10] Like fairy tales, these stories have formulaic characters and plots. This, Billman argues, is the strength of the mystery since they give their readers "clear cut 'data' about literary construction and narrative categories" (Billman, 35).

Alexander's Vesper books may seem predictable and stale to the adult who reads the *New York Times,* but they introduce a new mode of writing to the youngster who earlier read fairy tales and fantasies. Using the mystery format, Alexander encourages these young readers to predict the outcome of the story. His first person narrative forces the reader to consider the difference between the narrator and the author. Discussing the role of the storyteller in "Some Presumptuous Generalizations about Fantasy" Perry Nodelman says that "the secret of good fantasy is the control of tone—the creation through the right choice of words of the right relationship between the writer and his audience. The right relationship in a fantasy is the audience's faith in the narrator; the right words create a tone of matter-of-fact acceptance that allows us to believe in what we know does not exist."[11] Alexander's mysteries work in much the same way, but they demand a more sophisticated reader, one who has already learned the elements of formulaic writing and the role of the narrator. The Vesper books lend themselves to studies of reader response and its relationship to the author's implied messages, and they imply a need to consider how real reader, implied reader, and ideal reader response theory works in children's literature.

Worldwide Fame

It is impossible to deny Alexander's place in twentieth-century children's literature. His books have been translated in many languages, and his awards are from several countries. All of his books for adolescent readers, except the two early biographies, have remained in print, an indication of their popularity. He continues to hear from his real audiences through letters, phone calls, and classroom visits. Because he uses a variety of literary styles, his books appeal to varied audiences. Alexander never forgets who his first audience is: the youthful reader who wants a fast-moving story full of unusual personalities. However, he is aware of his secondary audience of teachers, librarians, and critics and talks openly to them about the art of writing and what it means to be a children's author.

Alexander has dared to innovate in order to bring alive past literary genres for twentieth-century children. Scholarly appraisals of his work should flourish as critical theory that looks at the various schools of criticism gains support in children's literature.

Lloyd Alexander's writings suggest the need for studies in the aesthetics of reception as advocated by critic Hans Robert Jauss. Jauss has suggested that critical appreciation depends upon acknowledgment of individual works in terms of their historical position and significance to the previous body of literature. Thus a new work can solve formal and moral problems that were left unanswered in previous writing and can suggest new problems for the writer and the critic.[12] Alexander's body of works points out that writers of children's literature need to be studied in more eclectic ways. The lack of critical discussion on Alexander's later writing suggests that today's critical studies in children's literature have not evolved beyond genre criticism. Alexander's works demand a different kind of discussion. Future discussions that approach the author for his literary position in children's literature can provide a new critical model that is less gender-burdened, more attentive to the variety of critical audiences in children's literature and that ultimately opens the way for discussing the individual needs of the various audiences to whom Alexander speaks.

Notes and References

Chapter One

1. *The Foundling and Other Tales of Prydain* (New York: Holt, Rinehart & Winston, 1973), 43.
2. "Seeing with the Third Eye," *English Journal*, May 1972, 36.
3. Anne Commire, *Something about the Author*, vol. 3 (Detroit: Gale Research, 1972), 8.
4. "Gertrude Stein," *Cricket*, January 1977, 58–59.
5. *Janine Is French* (New York: Crowell, 1958), 1.
6. "*SLJ* Meets Lloyd Alexander," *School Library Journal*, 15 April 1971, 1422.
7. "Wishful Thinking—Or Hopeful Dreaming?" *Horn Book*, August 1968, 386.

Chapter Two

1. *Borderhawk: August Bondi* (New York: Farrar, Straus & Cudahy, Jewish Publications Society, 1958), 15; hereafter cited in the text.
2. James L. Clifford, *From Puzzles to Portraits: Problems of a Literary Biographer* (Chapel Hill: University of North Carolina Press, 1970), 90–91.
3. *The Flagship Hope: Aaron Lopez* (New York: Farrar, Straus & Cudahy, Jewish Publication Society, 1960), 5; hereafter cited in the text.

Chapter Three

1. In *Children's Literature Review*, vol. 5, ed. Gerald J. Sennick (Detroit: Gale Research, 1983) Alexander comments, "I accumulated box after box of file cards covered with notes, names, relationships, and I learned them cold. . . . Nothing suited my purposes. At that point, the Muse in Charge of Fantasy, seductive in extremely filmy garments, sidled into my work room. 'Not making much headway, are you? How would it be,' she murmured huskily, 'if you invented your own mythology?

Isn't that what you really want?'" His entire discussion of his use of *The Mabinogion* is found in this volume, 14–15.

2. Lady Charlotte Guest, *The Mabinogion,* limited facsimile edition (Chicago: Academy University Press, 1978), 4; hereafter cited in the text.

3. *The Book of Three* (New York: Dell, 1964), 436–37; hereafter cited in the text.

4. "Substance and Fantasy," *Library Journal,* 15 December 1966, 6157.

5. *The Black Cauldron* (New York: Dell, 1965), n. p.; hereafter cited in the text.

6. *The Castle of Llyr* (New York: Dell, 1966), 7–8; hereafter cited in the text.

7. *Taran Wanderer* (New York: Dell, 1967), 12; hereafter cited in the text.

8. *The High King* (New York: Dell, 1968), 7; hereafter cited in the text.

9. *The Foundling and Other Tales of Prydain* (New York: Holt, Rinehart & Winston, 1973), 29.

Chapter Four

1. *My Five Tigers* (New York: Thomas Y. Crowell Co., 1956), 2; hereafter cited in the text.

2. *Time Cat: The Remarkable Journeys of Jason and Gareth* (New York: Holt, Rinehart & Winston, 1963) 8; hereafter cited in the text.

3. Dee Stuart, "An Exclusive Interview with Newbery Award–Winning Author Lloyd Alexander," *Writer's Digest,* April 1973, 58–59.

4. *The Cat Who Wished to Be a Man* (New York: E. P. Dutton, 1973), 4–5; hereafter cited in the text.

5. Alexander actually wrote two more stories to be included in *The Town Cats and Other Tales* that were subsequently excluded. One of the two was set in China, and it was later published in two parts by *Cricket* magazine. The second, set in Ireland, is on hold for an anthology.

6. *The Town Cats And Other Tales* (New York: E. P. Dutton, 1977), 36; hereafter cited in the text.

Chapter Five

1. *The King's Fountain* (New York: E. P. Dutton, 1971), no pagination. A part of my discussion on the book's conception draws from the

book's "About Author and Artist." The remaining elements come from my discussions with Lloyd Alexander.

2. Discussion of the book relies on an interview with Lloyd Alexander. *The Four Donkeys* (New York: Holt, Rinehart & Winston, 1972), no pagination. This second picture book was illustrated by Lester Abrams.

3. Mary Lou McGrew, *School Library Journal,* December 1972, 54.

4. Citations from *The Fortunetellers* are from Alexander's unpublished manuscript.

Chapter Six

1. Paul Heins, Review of *The Marvelous Misadventures of Sebastian, Horn Book Magazine,* December 1970, 628.

2. Zena Sutherland and May Hill Arbuthnot, with Dianne L. Monson and Dorothy M. Broderick, *Children and Books,* 7th ed. (Glenview, Ill.: Scott, Foresman, 1986), 234.

3. "*SLJ* Meets Lloyd Alexander," 14422–23.

4. *The Marvelous Misadventures of Sebastian: Grand Extravaganza, Including a Performance of the Entire Cast of the Gallimaufry-Theatricus* (New York: E. P. Dutton, 1970), 2; hereafter cited in the text.

5. Reviews for most of Alexander's books have been summarized in "Lloyd Alexander," in *Children's Literature Review,* vol. 5, ed. Sennick. The discussion here is based on that summary.

6. *The Wizard in the Tree* (New York: Dell Publishing, 1975), 119; hereafter cited in the text.

7. "A Personal Note on Charles Dickens by Lloyd Alexander," *Top of the News,* November 1968, 12–13.

8. "Fantasy as Images: A Literary View," *Language Arts* April 1978, 446.

9. *Children's Literature Review,* vol. 5, 24. Only one reviewer felt that the book was not successful. Barbara Wersba stated, "At this point in his career, it might be wise to leave the swashbuckling behind."

10. *The First Two Lives of Lukas-Kasha* (New York: Dell, 1982), 2; hereafter cited in the text.

Chapter Seven

1. M. Jean Greenlaw, "Profile: Lloyd Alexander," *Language Arts,* April 1984, 409.

2. Alexander continues his discussion of the historical representations in "Notes on the *Westmark Trilogy*," *Advocate* 4 (Fall 1984), concluding, "A fantasy? Sort of. Historical novel? Not really."

3. *Westmark* (New York: Laurel-Leaf, 1982), 9; hereafter cited in the text.

4. *The Kestrel* (New York: Laurel-Leaf, 1983), 13; hereafter cited in the text.

5. *The Beggar Queen* (New York: Laurel-Leaf, 1985), 128; hereafter cited in the text.

6. Correspondence with the author, 23 May 1982.

Chapter Eight

1. "Travel Notes," *Innocence & Experience: Essays & Conversations on Children's Literature*, ed. Barbara Harrison and Gregory Maguire (New York: Lothrop, Lee & Shepard Books, 1987), 195; hereafter cited in the text.

2. Mark Taylor, in his May 1964 review of *The Foundling and Other Tales of Prydain* for *Psychology Today* wrote, "The stories may be too short to achieve the power that the book-length chronicles generate" (20). Never a complimentary reviewer of his works, Barbara Wersba continually alluded to his earlier fantasy series in *New York Times Book Review*. Always, she suggested that he was less successful in his newest venture. Failing to see the new books as anything more than repeat performances, she said, "He must find new countries to explore" (4 May 1974) and advised that "it might be wise to leave the swashbuckling behind" (10 December 1978).

3. "High Fantasy and Heroic Romance," *Horn Book Magazine,* December 1971, 579.

4. "Where the Novel Went," *Saturday Review,* 22 March 1969, 62.

5. Robert Newsom, *A Likely Story: Probability and Play in Fiction* (New Brunswick, N.J.: Rutgers University Press, 1988), 144.

6. *The Illyrian Adventure* (New York: E. P. Dutton, 1986), 3; hereafter cited in the text.

7. *The Philadelphia Adventure* (New York: Children's Books, 1990), 147; hereafter cited in the text.

8. *The El Dorado Adventure* (New York: E. P. Dutton, 1987), 25; hereafter cited in the text.

9. *The Jedera Adventure* (New York: E. P. Dutton, 1989), 19; hereafter cited in the text.

10. *The Drackenberg Adventure* (New York: E. P. Dutton, 1988), 116; hereafter cited in the text.

Chapter Nine

1. John Rowe Townsend, "Heights of Fantasy," *Children's Literature Review* 5 (1983): 7–12.
2. C. W. Sullivan II, *Welsh Celtic Myth in Modern Fantasy* (New York: Greenwood Press, 1989), 56; hereafter cited in the text.
3. Barbara Z. Keifer, "Wales as a Setting for Children's Fantasy," *Children's Literature in Education,* Summer 1982, 96–97.
4. Laura Ingram, "Lloyd Alexander," *The Dictionary of Literary Biography,* vol. 52 (Detroit: Gale Research, 1986), 8–13; hereafter cited in the text.
5. Jack Zipes, "The Age of Commodified Fantasticism: Reflections of Children's Literature and the Fantastic," *Children's Literature Association Quarterly* (Winter 1984–85): 188; hereafter cited in the text.
6. James S. Jacobs, "A Personal Look at Lloyd Alexander," *Advocate* (Fall 1984): 8–18.
7. Lois Kuznets, "High Fantasy in America: Alexander, LeGuin and Cooper," *The Lion and the Unicorn* 9 (1985): 30.
8. Jon C. Stott, "Lloyd Alexander's Chronicles of Prydain: The Nature of Beginnings," in *Touchstones: Reflections on the Best in Children's Literature,* vol. 1. ed. Perry Nodelman (West Lafayette, Ind.: ChLA Publications, 1985).
9. Susan Isaacs, review of *The El Dorado Adventure, New York Times Book Review,* 7 June 1987.
10. Carol Billman, "The Child Reader as Sleuth," *Children's Literature in Education* (Spring 1984): 33; hereafter cited in the text.
11. Perry Nodelman, "Some Presumptuous Generalizations about Fantasy," *Festschrift: A Ten Year Retrospective* (West Lafayette, Ind.: ChLA Publications, 1983), 27.
12. Hans Robert Jauss, *Toward an Aesthetic of Reception,* trans. Timothy Bahti (Minneapolis: University of Minnesota, 1982), 32.

Selected Bibliography

Primary Works

Books for Children and Young Adults

The Beggar Queen. New York: Dell Publishing Co., 1984.
The Black Cauldron. New York: Dell, 1965.
The Book of Three. New York: Dell, 1964.
Borderhawk: August Bondi. New York: Farrar, Straus & Cudahy /Jewish
  Publication Society, 1958.
The Castle of Llyr. New York: Dell, 1966.
The Cat Who Wished to Be a Man. New York: E. P. Dutton, 1973.
Coll and His White Pig. New York: Holt, 1965.
The Drackenberg Adventure. New York: E. P. Dutton, 1988.
The El Dorado Adventure. New York: E. P. Dutton, 1987.
The First Two Lives of Lukas-Kasha. New York: Dell, 1978.
The Flagship Hope: Aaron Lopez. New York: Farrar, Straus & Cudahy,
  Jewish Publication Society, 1960.
The Foundling and Other Tales of Prydain. New York: Holt, Rinehart &
  Winston, 1973.
The Four Donkeys. New York: Holt, Rinehart & Winston, 1972.
The High King. New York: Dell, 1968.
The Illyrian Adventure. New York: E. P. Dutton, 1986.
The Jedera Adventure. New York: E. P. Dutton, 1989.
The Kestrel. New York: Laurel-Leaf, 1983.
The King's Fountain. New York: E. P. Dutton, 1971.
*The Marvelous Misadventures of Sebastian: Grand Extravaganza, in-
  cluding a Performance of the Entire Cast of the Gallimaufry-
  Theatricus.* New York: E. P. Dutton, 1970.
The Philadelphia Adventure. New York: Dutton's Children's Books, 1990.
Taran Wanderer. New York: Dell, 1967.
Time Cat: The Remarkable Journeys of Jason and Gareth. New York:
  Holt, Rinehart & Winston, 1963.
The Town Cats and Other Tales. New York: E. P. Dutton, 1977.
The Truthful Harp. New York: Holt, 1967.

Westmark. New York: Laurel-Leaf, 1982.
The Wizard in the Tree. New York: Dell, 1975.

Unpublished Children's Book Manuscript

The Fortunetellers. Copy from Lloyd Alexander.

Articles

"Fantasy as Images: A Literary View." *Language Arts*, April 1978, 440–
46. Discusses how fantasy authors use imagery to create a sense of
reality.
"Gertrude Stein." *Cricket* January 1977, 54–59. Tribute to Stein recalling
their friendship.
"High Fantasy and Heroic Romance." *Horn Book Magazine*, December
1971, 577–84. Talks of the mimetic elements in the hero's tale found
in classical literature and in contemporary high fantasy.
"Identifications and Identities." *Wilson Library Bulletin*, October 1970,
144–48. Discusses how past authors have used history in their writing and suggests that literature can help the reader identify with
those who are different from himself.
"No Laughter in Heaven." *Horn Book Magazine*, February 1970, 11–19.
Begins with a discussion of his early adult writing and continues
with an explanation of the need for humor in realism.
"Notes on the *Westmark Trilogy*." *Advocate* 4 (Fall 1984): 1–6. Explains
that the French Revolution is an essential ingredient in his development of the series' setting and characterization.
"On Responsibility and Authority." *Horn Book Magazine*, August 1974,
363–64. A call for the fiction author's freedom from censorship.
"A Personal Note on Charles Dickens by Lloyd Alexander." *Top of the
News*, November 1968, 10–14. Discusses Dickens's greatness in
terms of his ability to treat fundamental social issues.
"Seeing with the Third Eye." *English Journal*, May 1972, 35–40. An ad-
dress given at NCTE's Books for Children luncheon, which begins
by discussing his early education. Throughout, Alexander suggests
that reader response depends on audience reception and
participation.
"Substance and Fantasy." *Library Journal*, 15 December 1966, 6157–59.
An explanation of how he used the Welsh legends in writing the
Prydain series.
"Truth about Fantasy." *Top of the News*, January 1968, 168–74. Discusses
the differences between folklore and fantasy and suggests that the

fantasy author creates a story with two meanings, one that is at the plot's surface and one that is deeper, more philosophical.

"Where the Novel Went." *Saturday Review,* 22 March 1969, 62. Talks of the qualities found in good children's literature.

"Wishful Thinking—or Hopeful Dreaming?" *Bookbird* 7 (1969): 3–9. (Reprinted from *Horn Book Magazine,* August 1968, 383–90.) Discusses the meaning of fantasy and the differences between adult and children's literature.

Adult Books

And Let the Credit Go. New York: Thomas Y. Crowell Co., 1954.
Janine Is French. New York: Crowell, 1958.
My Five Tigers. New York: Thomas Y. Crowell Co., 1956.
My Love Affair with Music. London: Cassell & Company, 1960.

Secondary Works

Books

Clifford, James L. *From Puzzles to Portraits: Problems of a Literary Biographer.* Chapel Hill: University of North Carolina Press, 1970.

Coates, Paul. *The Realist Fantasy: Fiction and Reality since "Clarissa."* New York: St. Martin's Press, 1983.

Eames, Hugh. *Sleuths, Inc.: Studies of Problem Solvers Doyle, Simenon, Hammett, Ambler, Chandler.* Philadelphia: J. B. Lippincott, 1978.

Grossvogel, David I. *Mystery and Its Fictions: From Oedipus to Agatha Christie.* Baltimore: Johns Hopkins University Press, 1979.

Guest, Lady Charlotte. *The Mabinogion.* Limited facsimile edition. Chicago: Academy University Press, 1978.

Harrison, Barbara, and Gregory Maguire, eds. *Innocence & Experience: Essays & Conversations on Children's Literature.* New York: Lothrop, Lee & Shepard Books, 1987.

Hearne, Betsy, and Marilyn Kaye, eds. *Celebrating Children's Books.* New York: Lothrop, Lee & Shepard Books, 1981.

Jauss, Hans Robert. *Toward an Aesthetic of Reception,* translated by Timothy Bahti. Minneapolis: University of Minnesota, 1982.

Newsom, Robert. *A Likely Story: Probability and Play in Fiction.* New Brunswick, N.J.: Rutgers University Press, 1988.

Said, Edward W. *The World, the Text and the Critic.* Cambridge: Harvard University Press, 1983.

Searles, Baird, Beth Meacham, and Michael Franklin. *A Reader's Guide to Fantasy.* New York: Facts on File, 1982.

Sullivan C. W., III. *Welsh Celtic Myth in Modern Fantasy.* New York: Greenwood Press, 1989.

Tynn, Marshall B., Kenneth J. Zahorski, and Robert H. Boyer. *Fantasy Literature: A Collection and Reference Guide.* New York: R. R. Bowker, 1979.

Articles

Billman, Carol. "The Child Reader as Sleuth." *Children's Literature in Education* (Spring 1984): 30–41. Critical discussion of the mystery genre in children's literature.

Carr, Marion. "Classic Hero in New Mythology." *Horn Book Magazine,* October 1971, 508–13. Shows how Alexander has brought the mythic hero alive, using the analysis of Jan de Vries as the basis for comparison.

Durell, Ann. "Who's Lloyd Alexander?" *Horn Book Magazine,* August 1969, 382–84. Describes Alexander as an author who uses his life in his stories.

Greenlaw, M. Jean. "Profile: Lloyd Alexander." *Language Arts,* April 1984, 406–13. Transcript of an interview with Alexander in an elementary school classroom. The questions are typical of Alexander's youthful readers.

Ingram, Laura. "Lloyd Alexander." In *Dictionary of Literary Biography,* vol. 52, 3–21. (Detroit: Gale Research, 1986.) Evaluates all of Alexander's published works through 1986.

Jacobs, James S. "A Personal Look at Lloyd Alexander." *Advocate* (Fall 1984): 8–18. Detailed biographical sketch of Alexander, which includes an autobiographical explanation of Alexander's willingness to share information and ideas with Jacobs.

Kiefer, Barbara Z. "Wales as a Setting for Children's Fantasy." *Children's Literature in Education,* Summer 1982, 95–101. A discussion of Alexander's and Susan Cooper's settings in their high fantasy series.

Kuznets, Lois. "High Fantasy in America: Alexander, LeGuin and Cooper." *The Lion and the Unicorn* 9 (1985): 19–35. Interprets the reader's response to the three authors from an American feminist viewpoint.

May, Jill P. "Lloyd Alexander's Truthful Harp." *Children's Literature Association Quarterly* (Spring 1985): 37–38. Biographical sketch, which concludes that Alexander has placed twentieth-century concerns in his writing.

Nodelman, Perry. "Some Presumptuous Generalizations about Fantasy." In *Festschrift: A Ten Year Retrospective,* 26-27. West Lafayette, Ind.: ChLA Publications, 1983. Discusses the storytelling element in fantasy in terms of the implied audience.

Omdal, Marsha DePrez. "For Wayfarers Still Journeying. . . ." *Language Arts,* April 1978, 501–2. Describes Alexander's Prydain characters as "very real people who deal directly with honest feelings and emotions."

Sennick, Gerald J., ed. "Lloyd Alexander." In *Children's Literature Review,* vol. 5, 13–26. Detroit: Gale Research, 1983. Includes author remarks, summaries of book reviews of Alexander's books up through Westmark series.

"*SLJ* Meets Lloyd Alexander." *School Library Journal,* 15 April 1971, 1421–23. Discussion of the events and characters in Alexander's *The Marvelous Misadventures of Sebastian.*

Stott, Jon C. "Lloyd Alexander's Chronicles of Prydain: The Nature of Beginnings." In *Touchstones Reflections on the Best in Children's Literature,* vol. 1, 21–29. West Lafayette, Ind.: ChLA Publications, 1985. Lucid discussion of Alexander's use of the bildungsroman pattern in the Prydain books.

Stuart, Dee. "An Exclusive Interview with Newbery Award–Winning Author Lloyd Alexander." *Writer's Digest,* April 1973, 33–35, 57–58. Alexander answers questions about his work habits, his philosophy toward writing for children, and fantasy as a genre.

Sutherland, Zena. "Captive Author, Captivated Audience." *Saturday Review,* 22 April 1972, 78. Report of a meeting between children and Alexander at the University of Chicago's Laboratory School.

Townsend, John Rowe. "Heights of Fantasy." *Children's Literature Review* 5 (1983): 7–12. Townsend compares Alexander's use of high fantasy elements to Tolkien, Patricia Wrightson, and Susan Cooper, and judges Alexander's work inferior.

Tunnell, Michael O. "Eilonwy of the Red-gold Hair." *Language Arts,* September 1989, 558–63. Considers Eilonwy the prototype of all later Alexander heroines.

Tunnell, Michael O., and James S. Jacobs. "Alexander's Chronicles of Prydain: 20 Years Later." *School Library Journal,* April 1988, 27–31. Retrospective tribute to Alexander's series, which discusses its place in children's literature.

Zipes, Jack. "The Age of Commodified Fantasticism: Reflections of Children's Literature and the Fantastic." *Children's Literature Association Quarterly* (Winter 1984): 187–90. Gives an overview of fantasy criticism and calls for fantasy that will "not cheapen human dignity, but form unique questions about why we have not become what we dream of becoming."

Index

163

The Author

Jill P. May is an associate professor at Purdue University where she teaches courses in children's and young adult literature. She is an active member of the Modern Language Association, the Children's Literature Association, the National Council of Teachers of English, and the Children's Literature Assembly. She initiated and coordinated ChLA's Symposium on Teaching Literary Criticism in the Elementary Schools and has served on NCTE's and CLA's curricula committees. She is the editor of *Children and Their Literature: A Readings Book* (1983) and author of *Film and Filmstrips for Language Arts: An Annotated Bibliography* (1981).

The Editor

Ruth K. MacDonald is a professor of English and head of the Department of English and Philosophy at Purdue University. She received her B.A. and M.A. in English from the University of Connecticut, her Ph.D. in English from Rutgers University, and her M.B.A. from the University of Texas at El Paso. To Twayne's United States and English Authors series she has contributed the volumes on Louisa May Alcott, Beatrix Potter, and Dr. Seuss. She is the author of *Literature for Children in England and America, 1646–1774* (1982).